Praise for *TRUE STRENGTH*...

"I am recommending this book to everyone I know!"
-Jon Gordon
16-Time International Bestselling Author of
The Energy Bus, Training Camp & *The One Truth*

"I thank you Todd, for this book, for years of sincere encouragement, and for all the lives you touch every day."
-Robin Sharma
International Bestselling Author and Advisor
Trusted By NASA, Nike, Starbucks & More

"*TRUE STRENGTH* is a powerful playbook for overcoming life's toughest challenges. Todd's story will inspire you to lead with faith and courage, both on and off the field."
-Tony Dungy
Super Bowl-winning Head Coach
and *New York Times* Bestselling Author

"*TRUE STRENGTH* is not just a story of overcoming obstacles; it's a manual for living a life filled with purpose, meaning, and happiness, despite the inevitable challenges we face. Forging strength takes serious work—but it's well worth the reward."
-Arthur C. Brooks
Professor
Harvard Kennedy School & Harvard Business School
and #1 *New York Times* Bestselling Author

"In *TRUE STRENGTH*, Todd allows us to see the depth of his character—a blend of toughness and faith that has inspired me both on and off the field."

-Drew Brees
Super Bowl Champion and MVP & 13-Time Pro-Bowler

"Todd Durkin has always been an open book to those closest to him. With *TRUE STRENGTH*, he extends that openness to the world, sharing guarded secrets and stories that will change your life, as they have mine."

-LaDainian Tomlinson
Pro Football Hall of Famer & NFL MVP

"As an author, I know that the best books are the ones that change us from the inside out. *TRUE STRENGTH* is one of those rare gems, offering a transformative journey of resilience and self-discovery."

-Rory Vaden
Cofounder of Brand Builders Group
and *New York Times* Bestselling Author of *Take the Stairs*

"As a physician, I know that true healing requires more than just physical recovery. *TRUE STRENGTH* is a powerful reminder that our mental and emotional resilience are just as crucial for overcoming life's challenges."

-Dr. Gabrielle Lyon
Author of the *New York Times* Bestselling Book, *Forever Strong*

"Like Todd, this book is a force of nature."

-Kostas "Gus" Cheliotis
Co-Founder & COO
Nassau Financial Group

"*TRUE STRENGTH* is an incredible testament to God's strength and power... and as someone who saw what Todd went through first-hand, a testimony of Todd's unwavering determination and faith."

-Miles McPherson
Senior Pastor of The Rock Church and
Bestselling Author of *The Third Option*

"Thanks to Todd's incredible gift for bringing out the best in people, *TRUE STRENGTH* is like a superfood for your soul. Packed with the perfect blend of heartfelt inspiration and transformative practical advice, this book will make you feel your absolute best, even in the worst of times."

-Jeff Fenster
Founder of Everbowl and WeBuild

"Todd has repeatedly called me to be the best version of myself, as a father, husband, business leader, and friend. And this book, *TRUE STRENGTH*, will do the same for you, no matter the challenges and obstacles you face."

-John Teza
President & CEO
Hand and Stone Franchise Corp.

"*TRUE STRENGTH* makes you feel like a phoenix rising from the ashes. It will inspire you. Push you. And give you strength to carry through. Just as Todd has done for me, and so many others."

-Chad Michael Murray
Award-Winning Actor from "One Tree Hill"
and "A Cinderella Story"

"Todd's journey is a master class in resilience. This book will show you how to get back up after life knocks you down, again and again."

-Michael Chandler
Professional UFC Fighter &
3-Time Bellator Lightweight Champion

"Hollywood turned my life upside down. Then Todd Durkin helped me turn my life around again. Just like the difference-making stories I tell via film, *TRUE STRENGTH* will make a difference in your life. "

-Brian Presley
Actor, Writer, Director & Founder of P12 Films

"In *TRUE STRENGTH,* Todd shares his heart wrenching battle through adversity and pain. The lessons he learns on his journey are a reminder that 'true strength' is not merely about physicality. It is about the resilience of your soul. This book will bring you to tears, and then lift you and fill you with hope. In a world filled with pain and hardship, *TRUE STRENGTH* serves as a guiding light."

-Kelli Watson
Owner, Scriptor Publishing Group

"Instead of giving advice from the sidelines, Todd's coaching you from inside 'the arena.' That's why the personal stories and hard-won wisdom he shares in *TRUE STRENGTH* fire me up—and will fire you up, too!"

-Justin Prince
Global Entrepreneur, International Speaker,
& Bestselling Author of *Be the One*

"As an athlete, I know that the best coaches are those who lead by example. Todd does just that in *TRUE STRENGTH*: His story will move you, his authenticity will inspire you, and his resilience will leave you feeling unstoppable."

-Chase Daniel
14-Year NFL Quarterback & Super Bowl Champion

TRUE STRENGTH

A Memoir

31 Hard-Earned Lessons for
Overcoming Life's Most Turbulent Times

Todd Durkin
with **Clay Manley**

No part of this publication may be reproduced, stored in a retrieval system, or transmitted in any form or by any means—electronic, photocopying, recording, or otherwise—without prior written permission, except in the case of brief excerpts in critical reviews and articles. For permission requests, contact the author at todddurkin.com.

All rights reserved.

Copyright © 2024 Todd Durkin

ISBN: 9798327114593 (Paperback)
ISBN: 9798328144483 (Hardcover)

The author disclaims responsibility for adverse effects or consequences from the misapplication or injudicious use of the information contained in this book. Mention of resources and associations does not imply an endorsement.

Scriptor
PUBLISHING GROUP

Melanie, I couldn't have made it through the past four years, the hardest of my life, without you by my side. Your unwavering support, unconditional love, and inspiring words lifted me up when I was at my lowest. Thank you for being my rock, my inspiration, and my partner on this journey. And thank you for keeping it all together, while I struggled to do the same. Together, we'll reach "100 million."

Love,

Todd xo10

"The crest of the wave determines
the depth of the valley.
The depth of the valley determines
the crest of the wave."
-Dr. David Jeremiah

Contents

Foreword by Dr. David Jeremiah 1

Preface: The Origin of *TRUE STRENGTH* 5

Introduction: What to Expect 11

Prologue: Mexico 25

Chapter 1. Rest – Dodging Death 27
   Body – Schedule "Mellow Yellow" Time 40
   Mind – Listen to Lin-Manuel 41
   Soul – The Overworked Farmer 42

Chapter 2. Gratitude – Bad Knees, Full Heart 43
   Body – Walk It Out 50
   Mind – See Gratitude 51
   Soul – The Two Wolves 52

Chapter 3. Growth – My "Moment of Release" 53
   Body – Release Your "Anchor" 63
   Mind – The Paradox of Safety 64
   Soul – The Monkey and the Coconut 65

Chapter 4. Perspective – My Back and "The Conversation" .. 67
   Body – Leap the Line 80
   Mind – "Benefit Finding" 82
   Soul – There Must Be a Pony in Here 83

Chapter 5. Stillness – "The Letters" 85
    Body – The Most Difficult Exercise You Can Do 96
    Mind – The Neuroscience of Silence.. 97
    Soul – The Sound of One Hand Clapping 98

Chapter 6. Hope – A Hotel in Mexico and
                  Breaking the Cycle.. 99
    Body – Quarterback Your Healthset..109
    Mind – Quarterback Your Mindset 111
    Soul – Quarterback Your Soulset..112

Chapter 7. Presence – The Final Diagnosis 113
    Body – Get Off Your "But" 123
    Mind – Be Where Your Feet Are 124
    Soul – Stay in the Game..125

Chapter 8. Essence – What's Next? 127
    Body – Swim 134
    Mind – "Iron" Michael Chandler's Affirmation
            and My Favorite Quote..135
    Soul – The Candlelight Taoist Parable 136

Chapter 9. Faith – Connecting the "Coincidences"................. 137
    Body – Don't Wait to Listen...141
    Mind – Put on Your "Armor"..143
    Soul – Footprints in the Sand...144

And Then Some... 145
    Body – You Are Who You Surround Yourself With................145
    Mind – Find Your Sanctuary 149
    Soul – Serve Your Scars...150

The 31st Lesson... 151

A Note from the Co-Author 153

Foreword

By Dr. David Jeremiah

I will never forget the day I first walked into Todd Durkin's gym over a decade ago. I had just gone through some serious physical health issues and I was looking for help. What I got was help and a whole lot more!

First of all, I was intimidated. Lining the walls of Todd's gym are pictures of the people he has trained. It's like a who's who of the NFL and MLB. Todd will share many of his best practices with these famous athletes in this book, so I won't steal his thunder in this foreword. But hear me clearly, I did not belong in that group of people. If you ever visit Todd's gyms, you will not see my picture on the walls.

To this day, those pictures motivate me as I am reminded that the trainer who is helping me is the same one who has helped them. And that leads me to my second response: I am totally motivated... I mean more motivated than I can adequately describe. Todd's gyms are motivational centers with an atmosphere and energy that is palpable. I have often told my wife that if I were unable to work out physically, I would be helped greatly by just sitting in the gym for an hour and absorbing the spirit of hope and help that permeates that space. I have often shown up to the gym so tired and physically spent that I could not imagine working out. But somehow I seem to push through and on the way home, I always feel like a new man. Perhaps it is true that when you feel the least like working out, that is the time when working out is most needed.

And that leads me to the important message in this book. What Todd wants you to know is that *true strength* is more than lifting weights. That's why when people ask me why I love Todd Durkin and why I try to get as many training sessions with him as I can, I always answer with this statement: Todd Durkin trains people from the inside out. In other words, he knows and constantly communicates that *true strength* begins in your mind and in your heart, and only then can it be truly demonstrated in your body. You can't be in Todd's presence for very long before he is telling you to get your mind right.

Every time I hear that famous Todd Durkin phrase, I am reminded that the concept actually originates in the Bible: "As he thinks in his heart, so is he" (Proverbs 23:7). An anonymous author explained this concept in these terms: "Whatever you hold in your mind will tend to occur in your life. If you continue to believe as you have always believed, you will continue to act as you have always acted. If you continue to act as you have always acted, you will continue to get what you have always gotten. If you want different results in your life or your work, all you have to do is change your mind."

Here's another take on this: "You are not what you think you are, but what you think—you are!"

That statement is at the core of this book, *TRUE STRENGTH*. You are not just a body to work out in a gym. You are body, soul, and spirit. C. S. Lewis once wrote that "our bodies and our souls

Foreword

live so close together that they catch each other's diseases." In other words, you can't get your body right unless you get your mind right. Todd Durkin knows this, and it would not surprise me if someday up in heaven I am told about Todd's homegoing and that he had "Get Your Mind Right" etched on his tombstone.

During a particularly rough stretch in Todd's journey that is detailed in this book, I shared a quote with him that had been on my mind: "The crest of the wave determines the depth of the valley. And the depth of the valley determines the crest of the wave." Little did I know just how much Todd needed to hear these particular words, let alone how much I would come to rely on the truth of those words in the months ahead.

As I write this foreword, I am battling a serious disease called Transverse Myelitis. For nine months now, I have been trying to recover the strength in my legs, facing my own deep "valley." There are many days when I have to over-rule my body just to get out of bed. I've needed *true strength* to negotiate every single day. I think this is what the apostle Paul had in mind when he wrote, "I discipline my body and keep it under control" (1 Corinthians 9:27). If you know anything about diseases like Myelitis, you know that recovery is not linear. It's two steps forward and one step back. Only *true strength* can get you through those ups and downs.

I am sure you will not be surprised to learn that my *true strength* begins with my relationship with Jesus Christ. I truly believe "I can do all things through Christ who strengthens me" (Philippians 4:13). I recommend Him to you, and no matter who you are or where you are in life, I urge you to read Todd's book and discover that, whatever you are going through right now, *true strength* can be yours each day.

Friend, if you're facing challenges in your own life, if you're ready to break through to a new level of strength and resilience, then the message of TRUE STRENGTH is for you. In the pages of this book, Todd will guide you on a journey of transformation, showing you how to build unshakable strength from the inside out. The path ahead may be difficult, with inevitable "valleys" along the way, but when you learn to master your inner world, you can withstand and overcome any external challenge.

Dive into these pages with an open mind and an open heart. Absorb the wisdom and strategies Todd shares and begin to apply them in your own life. As you do, I am confident that you'll discover a strength and resilience beyond what you ever thought possible. When you cultivate your own *true strength*, there's no limit to the waves you can ride or the impact you can make. Let TRUE STRENGTH be your guide through the "valleys" and to the "crests." You'll soon discover that whatever you are going through right now, *true strength* can be yours each day... and this book can give you the help you're looking for and a whole lot more!

God bless you,

David Jeremiah

Senior Pastor,
Shadow Mountain Church
& Turning Point Ministries
NY Times Best-Selling Author

Todd and Dr. Jeremiah at FQ10

Preface

The Origin of *TRUE STRENGTH*

I never planned to write this book, literally. I said no to this exact title, *TRUE STRENGTH*, in 2010.

The New Orleans Saints were hoisting the Lombardi trophy after winning Super Bowl XLIV. Quarterback Drew Brees was the talk of every town. And rightfully so. Brees' career was supposed to be over, done, four years ago. He'd been let go by the San Diego Chargers almost four years to the date, after a devastating shoulder injury wrecked his throwing arm. At the time of his release, Brees couldn't toss a football even 10 short yards; for perspective, plenty of Pee Wee QBs can sling it twice as far.

Yet four years later, in 2010, Brees was the big winner of *the* big game: A Super Bowl champion *and* the Super Bowl MVP. And in the media storm that followed the Saints' Super Bowl victory, Brees was tossing my name around as a key member of his comeback team: Todd Durkin. His trainer. *The* trainer who got his body, mind, and soul right following that "career-ending" shoulder injury just a few short years earlier.

And then my phone rang. And rang. After being rejected by multiple publishers pre-Super Bowl, a plethora of them were interested in sharing my story post-Super Bowl. Brees' remarkable victory, his 2010 crest, ushered in a crest of my own: I finally had the opportunity to achieve my goal of writing a life-transforming book. A necessary step, one of many, to achieve my ultimate dream, my mission, of *impacting* 10 million lives.

With a sweep of my wrist, I signed on the dotted line of a book deal, my first, like a bat out of hell. (I wasn't going to wait and risk the project getting sacked. Back in 2010, self-publishing wasn't much of a thing. Authors wrote books. Fitness trainers did not.)

Then I started penning *The IMPACT Body Plan*, my magnum opus, with the world-class team at Rodale Books. To my delight, Rodale was the behemoth behind *Men's Health* and several other iconic fitness publications of the time. Through IMPACT, I could *impact*. Writing *The IMPACT Body Plan* felt like slinging the pigskin in my very own Super Bowl.

Experienced authors, which I was not, often require an entire year (or more) to craft a manuscript. A rookie like me? Writing on top of running a gym, Fitness Quest 10, open almost all hours of the day... training dozens of clients, from pros like Drew Brees and Darren Sproles to "Joes" like 70-year-old Donna Dickinson and my guy, insurance agent Ken "Sawman" Sawyer, morning, noon, and night... AND raising not one, not two, but three young children? I figured I'd need at least a year to whip up *The IMPACT Body Plan* (and a miracle, to boot).

Rodale gave me 10 weeks. *IMPACT* was a rush job. To capitalize on the Super Bowl hoopla, Rodale was determined to release the book by kickoff of the following NFL season. I was determined to seize the opportunity by writing the best book I possibly could, so I began writing every chance I could to meet Rodale's deadline.

Preface

Ten weeks later, the president of Rodale, the head honcho, requested an in-person meeting with me mere days before *IMPACT* was set to print. In essence, the only thing left to do was to select the perfect shade of neon yellow for the cover.

I remember boarding the cross-country flight from San Diego to New York City, beaming. *Man, they must have BIG plans for The IMPACT Body Plan!* I thought. *Let's go, baby!* Five hours later, when the plane touched down in the Big Apple, an ear-to-ear smile was still lighting up my face. I was buzzing with excitement, dreaming of the possibilities, outlining an entire sequel in my head.

I floated through the doors of the tower that housed Rodale. Then aboard an elevator soaring to the top of the building, where the big wigs overlooked the city that never sleeps. Then, as I rounded the corner to the president's office—a glass fishbowl—it appeared my dream had come true: A sequel!

Copies of a blue book cover, with my face on it, were plastered across the office windows. It was as if Rodale's president himself was carefully considering the perfect shade of royal blue for the sequel's cover. *Dreams do come true*, I thought! *Or do they?*

To my surprise, that royal blue book cover wasn't a sequel... it was a replacement. I guess I could be sold on a new color for *The IMPACT Body Plan*. After all, blue is my favorite color. But that wasn't the problem. The problem was that Rodale intended to replace the title, too. The heart of the book. The piece I was most passionate about. *How can I impact without IMPACT?*

To my dismay, the president himself had pulled rank. He'd ix-nayed the title, *The IMPACT Body Plan*, at the 11th hour. He must have known, or been informed, how attached I was to that word, *IMPACT*, hence the decision to fly me out and deliver the bad news in person.

"Impact..." he said, "sounds like a car crash."

Ugh. I heard him, but I disagreed. Then at that moment, I saw it: Across every royal blue cover plastered on the wall, *The IMPACT Body Plan*, the title, my title, had been replaced with two unfamiliar words: *TRUE STRENGTH*.

TRUE STRENGTH?

"What do you think, Todd?"

TRUE STRENGTH? What the heck is TRUE STRENGTH!? I thought.

No disrespect, but this seemed like a gross breach of contract. I felt bewildered and betrayed at the same time. After 10 grueling weeks of pouring my heart and soul into *The IMPACT Body Plan*, that book, *IMPACT*, was my baby. Exchanging the title for two new words, let alone a pair of words I'd never even uttered together before—*TRUE STRENGTH*—was like dumping salt on the wound.

I hated that name!

Ah... but why would I put up a fight? I didn't have a leg to stand on. I was a first-time author, with zero background and zero experience. Landing that book deal with Rodale was like a practice squad player, who hadn't seen action all season, being thrust atop the depth chart for the playoffs: I should just be happy to be there. And I was. Truly.

But I still put up a fight.

And when I did, BAM! I was hit with an ultimatum: "No *TRUE STRENGTH*, no book." *TRUE STRENGTH* is the title... or Rodale pulls the plug. I believe "take it or leave it" were the president's exact words.

And just like that, it felt like my dream, my mission—to impact 10 million people—was being ripped away from me inches from the endzone.

So what do you think I did? What would you do?

My eyes narrowed as I looked directly into the president's eyes. And without any hesitation, I pulled the plug *for* him, *for* Rodale. "No IMPACT, no book," I said. Determined. Stubborn. Stupid? Call it what you want, I hit *him* with an ultimatum. BAM! Rodale could write IMPACT with me. Or TRUE STRENGTH without me.

Take it or leave it.

"Get me out of here," I muttered under my breath, as I hopped in a cab and raced to the Newark airport to catch the next flight home. For a nauseating five hours that felt like five days, I gazed out a tiny airplane window, my mind swirling with unanswered questions: *What was going to happen to my "baby?" Did I do all that work for nothing? Is IMPACT dead? Will I ever get another shot at this? What's next?*

I didn't know what was next. Nor did my agent when I informed him of what had happened in NYC. But I did know one thing: The title was a non-negotiable for me.

IMPACT, to me, was like the air I breathe—invisible, yet essential. Just as a musician cherishes a familiar guitar, or a chef treasures a family recipe, or a homeowner holds an emotional bond with their first home, I had that undeniable, emotional bond to IMPACT.

I thought about that breakneck, 10-week writing process. And it became clearer to me than ever before: IMPACT is who I am. *IMPACT* is what I do. 10 million people, 10 million lives, will be impacted by me one way or another—albeit, with or without *The IMPACT Body Plan*. I wasn't going to let anything, or anybody, take that from me. Not even Rodale.

Weeks later, on September 14, 2010, just as the NFL season kicked off, and Drew Brees and the New Orleans Saints began their quest to defend their crown, a neon yellow book penned by Todd Durkin—and published by Rodale, Inc.—hit stores and newsstands nationwide.

Its title? *The IMPACT Body Plan!*

We did it, baby!

Today, that bright yellow book, *The IMPACT Body Plan*, symbolizes a crest to me: One of many, a continuous set of them, that began rolling in a decade before its publication, and continued to roll in, wave after wave, long after.

Introduction

What to Expect

By 2010, my gym, Fitness Quest 10, had already outgrown itself... twice; routinely honored as one of America's Top 10 Gyms, that cozy, 2,000 square-foot, shag carpet-lined fitness facility I opened in 2000 had ballooned to more than 8,000 square feet across two separate buildings.

Before Drew Brees came in to train, San Diego Chargers running back LaDainian Tomlinson showed up. Then came Darren Sproles. Then Reggie Bush. Then Gerald McCoy. Aaron Rodgers. Chase Daniel. Tony Gwynn Jr. Chris Young. Will Venable. Nick Hundley. "Iron" Michael Chandler. And many, many more professional athletes. I've had the privilege of being the trainer of choice to dozens of pros from all four major sports and beyond, including NFL Champions, MVPs, and Hall-Of-Famers, World Series Champions, MMA Champions, X-Game medalists, and Olympians. They've all trained at Fitness Quest 10.

In the early 2000s, just as authors wrote books, athletes signed apparel deals. Kevin Durant, for instance, signed a seven-year contract with Nike in 2007. I signed a contract that same year when I scored a deal with an up-and-coming athletic apparel brand. In fact, the company had just opened its first retail store when it brought me onto its roster. Its name: Under Armour. Fitness Quest 10 was the first Under Armour–sponsored training facility in the world, and I was named head of the newly-formed Under Armour Performance Training Council at the time, too.

The crests kept coming.

A year after pioneering perhaps the fitness industry's first Mastermind group and filling it with hundreds of the best and brightest minds in our field, industry-wide accolades began to pour in: In 2004, the IDEA Health & Fitness Association celebrated my contributions by naming me Personal Trainer of the Year. The recognition didn't stop there; the American Council on Exercise (ACE) echoed this honor the following year. Winning Personal Trainer of the Year twice was like winning back-to-back MVPs.

Fast-forward to 2017 and I was honored with the big kahuna, the Jack LaLanne Award, symbolizing a profound legacy and impact within the fitness sphere. Receiving that award placed me among a distinguished roster of past winners, including Jane Fonda, Alberto "Beto" Perez (founder of Zumba), Tony Horton, and, in subsequent years, Chalene Johnson and Billy Blanks. Winning that Jack LaLanne Award was like being inducted into the Hall of Fame.

And guess what? The crests kept coming.

The Jack LaLanne Award wasn't my only trip to a hall of fame in 2017. LaDainian Tomlinson was enshrined into the Pro Football Hall of Fame in Canton, Ohio, that same year. I held back tears from my seat at the Tom Benson Hall of Fame Stadium, looking up at the podium, and locking eyes with "Dain" as he accepted the honor. When he received his bronze bust, my name

Introduction

echoed across the stadium and up in the stands as he gave me a "special thanks."

And I wasn't just traveling to Ohio, or even the Midwest, then. I found myself traveling the world. By 2017, I had delivered 300+ keynotes across five different continents.

Meanwhile, when things seemingly couldn't get any better, perhaps the biggest crest rolled in when a lifelong dream came true: I got the call to co-star on a primetime television series produced by Dave Broome of *Biggest Loser* fame. Around the same time I received word that I'd been nominated for the Jack LaLanne Award, the series titled *STRONG* aired on Thursday nights, nationwide on NBC. (And later, *STRONG* became a mainstay on Netflix.) Spoiler alert: I was one of just two trainers who made it to the end of the series, allowing me into the homes (and, hopefully, hearts) of millions of viewers. As if the experience wasn't already incredible enough, *STRONG* was co-produced by my childhood hero, Sylvester Stallone. A die-hard *Rocky* fan, meeting Sly was yet another crest.

As an award-winning fitness trainer, with an apparel deal, a book deal, and a TV spot, it felt like I had the Midas touch. It was crest after crest after crest from 2000 on. And then… CRASH!

I freefell to rock bottom. After nearly 25 years of the highest of highs, I experienced my lowest of lows. Potential "career-ending" lows. Troughs. Valleys. Pits. Pills. Pain. Defeat. Disappointment. A death threat. And more troughs. And more valleys. And more pits. And more, and more, and more… and how much more can one man take!? WHOOSH. *Breathe, Todd. Breathe.*

After all those crests, it was valley after valley. Crash after crash.

This book, *TRUE STRENGTH*, shines a light on those crashes. In the following pages, I'm going to grab you by the hand and take you down into the depths of the valleys that I secretly tumbled into—for the first time ever, sharing the depths of my despair in riveting detail. Said differently, after nearly 25 years of good, the following pages are dedicated to the bad and the ugly, as well as what's next.

What the heck is TRUE STRENGTH!?

In 2010, when I was blindsided by those two words from a glass fishbowl overlooking New York City, I couldn't tell you. But now... I can. Because I found it. I forged it. I fostered my *TRUE STRENGTH*. *Not* by choice, but by design. At my lowest of lows. The valleys I tumbled into are what equipped me to write this book and empowered me to finally share *TRUE STRENGTH* with you, some 15 years later.

Because it was in the valleys that I found new compassion, empathy, and understanding. I'm now older, wiser, and while decades past my physical prime—at 53-years-young—I've never felt *stronger*. I've never been more lit up for life. I've never been more prepared, more excited, for the next crest. For the best that's yet to come. And I'd be living a lie, the very definition of hypocrite, if I only coached you from the crests, rather than the valleys. If I only shared the highlights and not the lowlights.

So before we go on, a quick warning: This book is far different from any of my others. It's a purposeful confessional: A tell-all to ensure my suffering was of service.

Introduction

You're about to step behind the curtain and see the behind the scenes that so often goes unseen. You're about to hear my inner dialogue... and it may be jarring. It's going to sound quite different from what you're used to. I'm about to uncover secrets I've never shared, as I chronicle what I've privately referred to as a "half-decade of hell" publicly, for the first time. You're about to learn far more about me than perhaps you already know—and in doing so, I hope you learn far more about you, too.

My stomach is in knots. I'm nervous. A bit scared. Vulnerable. *Yeah, vulnerable.* I'm feeling more vulnerable than ever before. But, in my heart of hearts, I know this will benefit me: Sharing my pain, my trauma, my valleys, my scars, will be therapeutic. Cathartic. It will allow me to grieve for the greater good. (After all, we grieve by remembering, don't we?)

And perhaps more importantly, I know from experience that what I'm about to share will benefit you, the reader. Because though this book is far different, far deeper, than my past entries as an author, I know of the incredible impact any book can have.

For example, when he was just 32 years old, Adam Ferreri was diagnosed with stage IV cancer.

I didn't know Adam. But in some serendipitous twist of fate, he stumbled upon a certain book at a hospital out east, on the complete other side of the country from me: My first book, *The IMPACT Body Plan*.

And get this: Adam didn't just read *IMPACT*. He completed his own anti-cancer version of the 10-week *IMPACT* workout protocol—while in treatment. Adam exercised in the hospital hallways and stairwells, mustering up as much strength and stamina as he could between taxing rounds of chemotherapy, while blasting the *Rocky* soundtrack to give himself an added boost of motivation to keep fighting, to go another round.

I only know this because Adam wrote to me. Crediting that book, *my book*, for "keeping him alive."

Meanwhile, another stranger in another country was facing a different beast; Tyler was shackled in the mind prison of PTSD (post-traumatic stress disorder).

Anxiety and depression were Tyler's norm. These feelings were so dark, so intense, that the Canadian cop didn't just down up to 13 pills a day... Tyler took steps to take his own life on more than one occasion. The first, with his service weapon. The second, with a belt wrapped around his neck.

Soon after, Tyler sent a note to me: "Though we've never met, no one has inspired me, impacted me, or instilled more confidence in me than you. There have been two moments in my life where I did not think I'd see the next day, and I will no longer allow myself to reach that space...

Mr. Durkin, Todd, please know that your videos, your WOWs, your Dose of Durkins, *your books*, and most importantly, the sound of your voice inspiring others has been the greatest support that I've found outside of my mental health professionals. You've been a HUGE part of giving my son his father back. For this, I love you as a brother." (I love you too, Tyler.)

Like I told him, he's why I do what I do.

It's amazing how sometimes you don't know when and where you're going to have an impact on someone. Adam and Tyler are just a few of many examples. It's stories like these, like theirs, that motivate me to keep serving. Keep sharing. Keep *writing*.

Some stories are shared in public, others kept in private. Some I've heard in the trenches of Fitness Quest 10. Others in

Introduction

passing. Some are just as extreme. I've been told my words, my books, have helped people survive abuse. Addiction. Diagnoses. Divorce. Financial ruin. Personal ruin. And more. And not just survive, but just as Adam and Tyler did, even thrive in the aftermath of these obstacles.

Others are far less extreme. Maybe my words have given you the motivation or inspiration to work out, shed some weight, hug a loved one a smidge tighter or a second longer, pursue a goal, dream bigger, eat better, or even share your story with the world, or your world. Maybe my words have guided you out of a rut, got you unstuck, or helped you reclaim your missing mojo. Or maybe they've given you hope, a friend, or a confidant—when you've needed these things most. Maybe some of my mantras now live in your head—making you more positive, more grateful, more present, more excited than you were before.

Humbly, any impact my words have had means the world to me. And I hope *TRUE STRENGTH* brings more of the same... and introduces more that's, well, different.

Because ironically, I didn't find my *TRUE STRENGTH* through my previous entries as an author. Nor will you. Forget *The IMPACT Body Plan*—my body was broken. Literally. That word, BROKEN, is scribbled inside my brown leather-bound journal—my tear-stained diary from the past half-decade—dozens of times. Every time I wrote "I'm broken," guess what? I was.

Get Your Mind Right? As you'll see in just a second, that was harder for me than ever before. In fact, my inner dialogue is perhaps the scariest to share. After all, I'm *the Get Your Mind Right* guy. And my mind was all wrong. *New York Times* bestselling author Jon Gordon once said, "Todd could motivate a rat into a mousetrap." But what happens when I'm the one trapped?

And *The WOW Book*—the one filled with what I call "soul fuel?" It might as well have been written by someone else. The soul had been sucked out of me like I'd come face to face with a dementor from my youngest son's favorite series, *Harry Potter*.

I'd never felt more empty. Or more lost. Or more defeated. Or more betrayed. Or more burned-out. Or more depressed. Or more confused. Or more hurt. Or more hollow—than I did from 2020-2023.

How about you?

Maybe you've been derailed by a diagnosis... or maybe someone you love has. Maybe you have your own pain... or you're feeling theirs. Maybe a devastating injury has taken hold of you. Or a divorce. A split. A life-altering change of some kind is crippling you now. Maybe it's a career change. Maybe you're in the midst of a midlife crisis, seeking change. Maybe you're stuck in a rut. Feeling like you can't catch a break. Or facing another kind of crisis. Your own head prison of sorts. Maybe you're feeling lost. Alone. Confused. Uncertain. Overwhelmed. Unfulfilled. Or maybe you're searching. Stirring. Stewing. Or perhaps you're fried. Frustrated. Fearful. Fatigued. Exhausted. Empty. Burned-out.

I've been there.

And I hope my vulnerability in the following pages is of tremendous value. I hope this book gives you understanding. Empathy. Solace. Inspiration. Compassion. Connection. Healing. Comfort. Resilience. And so much more—when you need it most. This book is designed to help you see the sun through the clouds. The forest for the trees. And to give you hope to help you cope. I hope reading these words brings you relief, and healing, and grieving, and so much more.

Introduction

    Whatever valley you're facing, my hope is this book will be all of that—and then some—for you. That through these pages you will find, forge, and foster the *TRUE STRENGTH, your TRUE STRENGTH*, to climb back up to your feet. And that this book will be like the sherpa that ushers you out of the valley and upwards… to your next crest. My intention is to share my bad and ugly to propel you through your bad and ugly.

    My hope is that after reading cover to cover, you, the reader, refer to this book as a lifeline. A saving grace. Or even a lifesaver. Maybe you're searching for something more. Something different. Or something even greater in life. I believe this book could be your guiding light. Illuminating your path to exactly that. Maybe you're reading purely for pleasure. Oh yeah, you'll get that too. But why not benefit from it? This book could be the key that unlocks an unexpected "aha" moment, turning point, or breakthrough for you. And if this book fell into your lap, well, I believe that nothing is by coincidence.

    Keep going. Keep reading. If you uncover just one golden nugget from this, it will be worth it. And I anticipate you'll uncover more than that. Thirty-one to be exact.

    Everyone has something. That's universal. We all face setbacks. Tough times. Valleys. The following pages reveal mine, as well as the ways I made progress, so you can do the same. The following is truly a tell-all experience, surfacing untold chapters of my story from a half-decade of hell. And more importantly, the hard-won lessons from my most trying and turbulent times.

    As you'll soon see, *TRUE STRENGTH* is like the phenomenon of eccentric strength, the 50% extra found on the way down. The "negative." During eccentric phases of movement—such as lowering a dumbbell in a bicep curl, descending into a squat, or the downward phase of a push-up—science, and experience, shows your body can handle up to 50% more weight than during the opposite, the lifting (concentric), or upward, phase of movement. This proves we're actually stronger, and our strongest, at our lowest. Whether you're a pro or a "Joe," you have this capability—to find new strength, added strength, at your weakest. And I'm going to help you unlock it.

In 1955, the comprehensive Kauai Study began tracking the lives of every child born on the Hawaiian island that year, following each of their journeys through adulthood, while focusing on those who encountered formidable challenges, or valleys, along the way—poverty, familial discord, and health issues among them.

This groundbreaking study shaped the field of psychology and resilience research and coined the term "protective factors." It uncovered, and proved, that those who *thrive* in the presence of adversity have a specific set of conditions or attributes that, when present, promote well-being despite adverse circumstances. While many struggled in the face of adversity, those with the right protective factors flourished. Those protective factors guided them to that extra 50%, that eccentric strength, that made them stronger on the other side. The undeniable, otherworldly power of protective factors was proven to be true by the children of Kauai—each of whom faced valleys as personal as yours as decades ticked by.

Like getting your macros right in your diet, protective factors are the macros for *TRUE STRENGTH*... revealed in each chapter

INTRODUCTION

to give you the strength, *TRUE STRENGTH*, to power through the valleys... and to your next crest.

However, knowledge of these protective factors isn't enough. Knowing is never enough. I know this from decades of training, coaching pros and Joes, from Olympians to entrepreneurs, moms and dads, grandmas and grandpas, fitness enthusiasts and weekend warriors, and everyone in between.

That's why, at the end of each chapter, I will coach you, showing you how to put these protective factors into practice, by sharing three hard-earned lessons to help you find, forge, and foster each factor: One for the body, one for the mind, and one for the soul.

Said differently, this book is part memoir and part personal development: Each behind-the-scenes story, broken into chapters, illustrates a universal attribute, or "protective factor," of *TRUE STRENGTH* that applies to any personal valley you face. And each hard-earned lesson for the body, mind, and soul shows you how to develop that factor in your life.

Body

TRUE STRENGTH is strength that transcends the gym. That's why these body boxes do not focus on physical exercises. Instead, each holds an action step. A step that elicits forward momentum, or *progress*, in some way, shape, or form. A best practice for the worst of times. Let's start with an example: Read this book cover to cover. That's your first action step.

> ## Mind
> Here you'll find transformative short stories, thought-provoking quotes, and other forms of "brain fuel" to help foster each protective factor of *TRUE STRENGTH*. Or at the very least, feed you food for thought that will nourish you during the toughest of times. The goal of these mind boxes is to help you get your mind right even when things are wrong.

> ## Soul
> Soul is the essence of your being. Your energy. Your life force. It's who you are at your core. My great friend, Pastor Miles McPherson, uses this analogy to illustrate soul: Picture a glove. Your soul is the hand that fills that glove, giving it shape, form, and structure. Without your soul, the glove is empty. It's crumpled. Lying flat. Lifeless. These soul boxes will lift your spirit and your soul like no other. After all, *TRUE STRENGTH* is found—and forged—from the inside out.

Together, these best practices, wisdom, and insight will have an incredible, synergistic-like effect on your life. Making the whole greater than the sum of its parts.

Some 15 years after turning down this exact title, *TRUE STRENGTH*, here we are, here I am, in an unforeseen twist of fate following my most twisted, turbulent times, showing you how to

Introduction

find, forge, and foster *your TRUE STRENGTH*, and make the absolute most of it, so no valley is too low.

As you turn the page, I look forward to impacting the world, and *your* world, through TRUE STRENGTH. *Let's go, baby!*

Prologue
Mexico

They say the lower you go, the higher you can go. But how much lower could *I* go?

At perhaps my lowest, I was crumpled up in the fetal position on a cold, hard hotel room floor—in Mexico. Begging, pleading, my wife, Melanie, between the wet streams of tears running down my face, to hit the streets in an effort to score me some body-numbing painkillers.

Picture a 50-year-old, God-fearing father of three begging his wife of 20 years to hunt down pills, like a junkie negotiating with a dealer. That was me.

Then in a brief moment of clarity, rocking in excruciating pain, clutching my knees for dear life, my forehead pinned to them, my right side pressed on that unforgiving floor, I thought to myself: If only they knew... *if only you knew.*

Now you will.

Buckle up, my friend... it's gonna be a bumpy ride.

1

Rest – Dodging Death

June 2020

"You got a gun?" I whispered to the armed guard beside me, as I scanned the surroundings from my chair.

"Sure do," he murmured, his gaze dropping to his waistline as he gently patted his hip.

A crowd of 30-40 people in masks covering their nostrils, mouths, and chins, stood before us—family, friends, and a few strangers mixed in. My eyes darted to the unfamiliar faces, the eyes I didn't recognize, between each sweep of my wrist.

They had gathered around the folding table placed in front of my gym, Fitness Quest 10, united in celebration. There I was, pen in hand, autographing the pitch-black cover of my newest marquee book, *Get Your Mind Right*. Yet I struggled to celebrate that monumental moment as the darkness of the cover mirrored some of the dark thoughts swirling through my mind as *Get Your Mind Right* made its debut on June 2, 2020.

Does that date ring a bell? It was "Blackout Tuesday"—a day overshadowed by mourning. Ahmaud Arbery, Breonna Taylor, and George Floyd's deaths dominated the news, along with the mounting toll of COVID-19.

Meanwhile, I wondered if my own death was imminent. For the first time (and hopefully the last time), I found myself on the receiving end of a death threat. My offense? Voicing my support for a close friend and client.

In the days leading up to the release of *Get Your Mind Right*, my client's name was smeared across traditional sports media and social media. The comments had devolved from disrespectful to outright racist. As someone who had worked closely with this man for several years, I felt compelled to speak out. So I did. I crafted a comment, sharing my support and shedding light on the man I knew—not just the celebrity, but the human being behind the headlines. I posted it below one of the most damning social media posts about him, hoping to provide some perspective and balance to the conversation.

To my surprise, that simple comment ignited a firestorm. It was like tossing a match into a powder keg. Next thing I knew, my inbox was flooded with messages—some angry, some supportive. But one really stood out: A legitimate death threat. A threat I couldn't brush off. After some investigation, authorities discovered the person who threatened me was local, living in Southern California, like me. Therefore, they labeled my situation a "high-risk" one. Hence the armed guard beside me... and the loaded gun cradled in his hip pocket.

The irony was not lost on me—there I was, promoting my new book titled *Get Your Mind Right*, while the world was spiraling in several ways. At the time, fear was perhaps the only emotion filling the void in my head, an emptiness, or empty tank, I'd been wrestling with on and off for quite some time. That emptiness was mirrored by the vacant building behind me: My baby, Fitness Quest 10.

My team and I anticipated shuttering the doors of Fitness Quest 10 for one week... maybe two. "Two weeks, worst case," local officials assured us. Yet, as the second week of June approached, we were nearing 13 weeks, nearly 90 full days, of complete closure. In the heart of California's stringent "Purple Zone," while we remained off-limits, strip clubs were green-lit to open. *What the heck?*

All of it—the deaths, the death threat, the media, COVID, California's contradictions—was secretly gnawing at me. As each day ticked by, stuck in the dreaded "Purple Zone," I found myself being dragged deeper into an unfamiliar valley of emotions—frustration, worry, anger, fear, exhaustion, and an escalating pressure—as I continued to steer the ship, Fitness Quest 10, through the storm of closures, furloughs, and the great unknown. Our livelihood was under siege, affecting not just me but also the 42 families depending on us, my dedicated team, the extended family of hundreds of fitness professionals in my Mastermind groups, and our clients—the people we serve—as well as their clients. Plus, the fitness industry as a whole was hanging on by a thread. Heck, more than 9,000 fitness centers in the U.S. closed during this time, for good.

I refused to let Fitness Quest 10 be one of them.

To me, Fitness Quest 10 is the physical symbol of a 20-year crest. To others, it's "the stuff of legend."

Many of the legendary workouts hosted there started with LaDainian Tomlinson, who later became NFL MVP. Tomlinson brought in Drew Brees, a future Super Bowl-winning quarterback. Brees brought in Darren Sproles, who became one of the

NFL's all-time leaders in all-purpose yards. Word spread like a wildfire, attracting more and more professional athletes like cornerback Charles "Peanut" Tillman, tight end Zach Ertz, wide receiver Golden Tate, and more, and more, and more.

But Tomlinson, Brees, and Sproles, in particular, were workout maniacs. They pushed each other so hard, I'd have to pull the bright red treadmill plug to stop them from one-upping each other in ferocious, session-ending sprints.

By June 2020, I needed someone to pull the plug for me.

When whispers of coronavirus started to spread, I was already burned-out. Empty. My tank was already below "E." I kept it to myself. After all, everybody has something. And I didn't want to give my pain a voice or project it on others.

―❦―

In 2017, not long after *STRONG* aired on NBC, I heard a whisper. "Yoo-hoo, Todd..." When you listen, you can hear whispers, too. They come from your conscience. Your inner voice. (Or, if you're like me, I choose to believe they come from a higher power. The man upstairs.) After the "honeymoon effect" of co-starring on *STRONG* wore off, that voice in my head began telling me I was built for something more, something different, something even greater.

I couldn't quite make it out at the time, but as I attempted to translate that whisper, it seemed it was suggesting the impossible: *Was it encouraging me to step away from Fitness Quest 10? No. That can't be it.* It was encouraging me to step away, in general. The whisper was a warning shot. It was telling me to rest, to recharge. Looking back, it was then—years before the pandemic, the deaths, and the death threat—that I started to feel the wave of that nearly 20-year crest—Fitness Quest 10, Under Armour, *The IMPACT Body Plan*, The Jack LaLanne Award, *STRONG*, etc.—beginning to break. And truthfully, so was I.

Competing on *STRONG*, against the world's fittest trainers, all of whom seemed to be half my age, wrecked my right shoulder. Shortly after my shoulder healed, my knee crumbled. I could barely walk. I couldn't exercise. So I went under the knife in 2018. Knee surgery: A replacement at just 48 years old. Another reminder... to slow down.

So what did I do? I sped up.

By 2019, I was beginning to flounder beneath that breaking wave. Gasping for air, while just barely treading water. Kicking with that bum knee. I could go on and on about the stirring of my soul, the constant fatigue, the crippling weight of exhaustion, the growing aches and pains, the rising flames of burn-out, all of which were working together, synergistically, to push me to the brink long before the pandemic, let alone "Blackout Tuesday," were a thing... but why? Why compare notes? Everybody has something.

Sproles retired in 2019. Brees contemplated it. Could I do the same?

Then BAM! In a weird way, the pandemic masked the flames of my burn-out. It masked the fatigue, the exhaustion, the strange sense of being "lost" despite my "success" in the fitness industry. It masked all my aches and pains, too. It, surprisingly, breathed new life into me. The worse things got, the more I chose to step up, even speed up. In a weird way, I loved it. The pandemic gave me a renewed rush of purpose that I hadn't felt since competing on *STRONG*.

Heck, *Get Your Mind Right* was supposed to come out months before "Blackout Tuesday" and days before the first confirmed case of COVID-19 in the U.S. was even reported. Perhaps the frustrating, publisher-produced delays were a blessing in disguise. Due to those delays, I was signing the cover of *Get Your Mind Right* when the world needed a jolt of positivity more than ever before, at the peak of the pandemic, when the "Purple Zone" had everyone seeing red.

I didn't just feel like 42 team members' families, hundreds of my TD Mastermind members' families, thousands of clients' families, and tens of thousands of extended family members needed me and my message. No. I felt like the entire world needed to get its mind right in the days, weeks, and months leading up to June 2020. And that refilled my "below-empty tank" with rocket fuel. Heck, I took to Zoom and social media, and hollered "Jump on my back... we got this." Literally. I said the same to my team and my Masterminders countless times. And perhaps, directly, or indirectly, to the world as well. I relished the role, the opportunity, to step up and play Superman for the industry I so loved. And to lift those in need outside of it.

In other words, the pandemic gave me a second wind.

Then that death threat took the wind out of my sails. It brought me crashing back down to earth. Back beneath my crashing wave.

While autographing those pitch-black book covers, I thought back to the process of writing *Get Your Mind Right*. I wrote that book as much for me as I did for you, the reader. There were countless times during the writing process, many moons before the pandemic, that my mind was wrong. The stirring. The fatigue.

Rest – Dodging Death

The exhaustion. The burn-out. The confusion. Rather than sharing my problems in the book, I wrote the book to solve them.

~~~

Perhaps my saving grace during that tumultuous, post-*STRONG* time period, leading up to the release of *Get Your Mind Right*, was my budding relationship with world-renowned pastor and founder of Turning Point Radio and Television Ministries, Dr. David Jeremiah. "Dr. J," as I like to call him, had taken his training to the next level prior to the pandemic, working out with me three days a week, as opposed to his usual one.

Let's face it: At age 77, Dr. J was past his prime physically. That was no secret. But he was still fit. Thin. Slender. The extra training sessions were paying off. He proved it one morning when I caught him flying on the treadmill. I remember thinking to myself, *Dr. J is cooking today! Let's go, baby!*

Picture a grey-haired, 77-year-old man sprinting like a 21-year-old Olympian. *He could give Tomlinson, Brees, and Sproles a run for their money this morning*, I thought to myself. I also thought, *Dang... the treadmill was only supposed to be our warm-up!*

Excited, I inched closer and closer to Dr. J. And as I did, he went faster and faster. *Keep leaning in, Todd! Keep leaning in!*

Then I looked up. And saw fear filling his eyes.

In a flash, I pulled the red emergency plug seconds before Dr. J could go flying off the treadmill. Turns out, I was to blame for the famed pastor's brush with the devil that morning. The very tip of my elbow had been resting directly on the treadmill's speed-up button. And every time I inched closer, every time I leaned in—tap, tap, tap—Dr. J *was* running faster... because my elbow was increasing the treadmill's speed.

My head sunk into my hands. *Did I almost just kill Dr. David Jeremiah?* Imagine... one of the world's most famous pastors—injured on my watch. Even worse, at my hands. (I could see the headline: "Durkin kills world-famous pastor, Dr. David Jeremiah, in treadmill accident.")

What would have happened if I hadn't pulled the plug? Picture it... Dr. J would have shot off the treadmill like Superman. Only he'd be flying in reverse—backwards, not forward.

Luckily, Dr. J has a fantastic sense of humor. "Some world-class training, huh, doc?" I asked. "Sometimes you gotta have someone else hit your speed up button, Todd," he quipped, as he caught his breath in the pauses between my profuse apologies. He was right. But the opposite is also true: You can't run a marathon at a sprinter's pace. Sometimes, we all need to slow down to the speed of life—me included.

~

Reminiscing about that treadmill incident with Dr. J takes me back even further, to a life-changing heart-to-heart I had with my "Yoda," Wayne Cotton, more than a decade prior, shortly after I opened the doors to Fitness Quest 10 back in 2000 and was, again, trying to be everything to everyone: "Hey Todd, is life a marathon or a sprint?" Wayne asked.

What's with the softball question, Wayne? Easy, I thought.

"Life's a marathon, Wayne!" I snapped back with a smile on my face and supreme confidence in my voice.

"Todd, you're dead wrong."

I am?

"Life is a *sprint*, Todd. A series of sprints. You've gotta sprint, recover, sprint, recover, sprint, recover," he explained. "It's no different from training your athletes. You gotta work them hard and then give them rest. You, Todd, are running a marathon at a sprinter's pace. You're not getting any rest!"

Funny how my training methods hadn't translated to my lifestyle. Back in 2000, I was trying to run a marathon at a sprinter's pace, growing a business that was bursting at the seams. Now, in June of 2020, I was attempting the same feat again—running a marathon at an all-out sprinter's pace, trying to save the same business and rescue my people, only with far more mileage on my body (and my mind). *One bad knee won't stop me!*

I recall Wayne closing that conversation with a grave warning: "If you keep it up, you could end up like your father," he said flatly as he looked me dead in the eye.

My dad died of a heart attack at just 58 years old. Wayne's words were a punch in the gut that left me dead in my tracks and covered in tears, because, deep down, I knew... he was right. A 2013 study published in the journal "Psychosomatic Medicine" found that individuals with high levels of burn-out are 79% more likely to be diagnosed with heart disease.

Like father, like son?

Yet nearly two decades after that come-to-Jesus conversation with Wayne, I was making the same mistake—again. Sprinting without rest. Speeding up, instead of slowing down. The world had stopped and I was going harder than ever.

Every world-class athlete requires rest to perform their best. That's why every sport has an "off-season." Heck, what do they prescribe when you're hurt? Rest. But what about you? What about me?

I knew I needed to slow down as I was signing those books with a watchful eye on the crowd. My body—and my mind—were craving rest and recovery. My business was hanging on by a thread. So was my health. And my mindset. I could feel it. I could hear it. Another whisper filled the void: "Recharge the ol' batteries before you run out of juice."

When I heard that whisper, the mountains filled my mind. *Go unplug in Telluride, Todd. Let your soul sing in the Smokies. Relax in Whitefish.* Yeah, Whitefish it is!

How long should I go for? A week? A month? A year? Years?

In that moment, I thought of Winston Churchill. And his "wilderness years."

In 1929, Churchill lost his position as a member of the government. He was exiled from office and retreated to his country home, Chartwell House, in England. There he devoted his time—entire years—to activities entirely outside the political sphere. He took up gardening, painting, and the like.

An entire decade later, Churchill returned to government at the outbreak of World War II, first as First Lord of the Admiralty and then as Prime Minister from 1940 to 1945.

It was in the 1940s, *after* his wilderness years, *after* his decade *away*, that Winston Churchill did arguably his best, most impactful, work.

His leadership, oratory skills, and determination were pivotal in bolstering British resolve during the darkest hours of World War II, from 1940-1945.

In other words, Winston Churchill's most famous speeches and soundbites… they came after 10 years of "rest."

Wilderness years? Sign me up.

In desperate need of a break a year or so before the book signing, I'd gone so far as to discuss the concept, to share Churchill's story, with Melanie while I was writing *Get Your Mind Right*. Instead of Churchill's wilderness years, how about a "sabbatical?" Melanie had taken a sabbatical from her college teaching job once, so she understood. She was game. We figured after *Get Your Mind Right* was released it'd be the right time to take a break. It could be the perfect opportunity to slow down.

But then, again, the pandemic happened. *Who needs a break?* (Wasn't it Churchill who said, "Never waste a good crisis?") Suddenly, I went from all but begging for a break to choosing to lead a "crusade"—a crusade I titled the "positivity pandemic" on social media.

I leaned into creating and sharing uplifting content through my channels, dubbing my daily series the "Good News Network." In this time of global despair and uncertainty, I felt we needed a daily dose of good news more than ever before. The "Good News Network" was intended to balance the narrative. It was dedicated to combating the rampant head trash and "stinking thinking" spreading as fast as the pandemic. It was like a bridge to *Get Your Mind Right*.

But balancing the narrative took a mental toll on me.

When the world hit the pause button, and everything we knew as normal was flipped upside down, I felt that deep in my soul. My gym, my sanctuary, where I pour my passion into helping others achieve their best selves, was suddenly out of bounds.

It was like someone, some cosmic force, had stripped me of the most critical part of my identity.

Imagine stepping into the gym, your sanctuary of strength and resilience, only to find the doors locked, the lights off, and silence where there used to be the comforting clank of weights and the steady rhythm of treadmills.

That isolation crushed me. The disconnect from my clients, my team, and my community hit me harder than I anticipated. I thrive on energy, connection, and the shared pursuit of greatness. To have that suddenly stripped away was a challenge like no other. Fatigued. Exhausted. Hurt. Burned-out. Now, isolated. Alone. Empty. Tack on a death threat, and I was on a downward spiral, spinning in a whirlwind of ugly emotions.

That's what the pandemic did to our daily lives; it turned everything off and left us in the dark. We went from high-fiving our teammates and hugging our loved ones to questioning if a simple handshake could put our lives at risk. Obviously, lives were lost—directly and indirectly. Two kids I coached died by suicide during that time. I wondered if I'd let them down. If I'd done enough. What more I could have done. I hurt for them and their families. I also couldn't help but think about my family. That could have been my kids. What if those were my kids?

Anger. Fear. Stress. Anxiety. Violence. It was the norm. I also felt the weight of responsibility. When you sign people's paychecks, you feel a certain sense of responsibility for their families and lives. Remember, we had 42 people on payroll at that time. I told them, I promised them, that I'd go down before the ship does. They didn't know I was already drowning.

Despite the doors of Fitness Quest 10 being closed, I kept going and going and going... until I was gone. Shortly after

Rest – Dodging Death

Blackout Tuesday, or as I called it, international *Get Your Mind Right* day, the Energizer bunny finally ran out of juice. (More on that later.)

From 2017-2020, I kept reloading—more, more, more—instead of "deloading"—less, less, less. Deloading is a term often used in strength and athletic training that applies to life. Tim Ferriss, the famed author of *The 4-Hour Workweek*, and the subsequent *4-Hour* series of bestselling books, refers to deloading as strategically taking your foot off the gas. In a 2016 blog entry titled *Why You Need a "Deloading" Phase in Life*, Ferriss shared that he "alternates intense periods of batching similar tasks (recording podcasts, clearing the inbox, writing blog posts, handling accounting, etc.) with extended periods of—for lack of poetic description—unplugging and messing around."

Churchill's wilderness years were his deloading phase. The off-season was Tomlinson's, Brees', Sproles', and the rest of the gang's deloading phase.

Ironically, I now know that *TRUE STRENGTH* requires a deloading phase, too. You have to unplug. You have to slow down… in order to speed up. As Dr. J would say, "When you're tired, you're not inspired."

I pulled the plug for Tomlinson, Brees, and Sproles many times. I pulled the plug for Dr. J, too. I did for others what I wouldn't do for myself. And by 2020, I was paying for it. I should have listened to the whispers.

Body

Schedule "Mellow Yellow" Time

Here's a practical way to pull the plug, or deload, courtesy of my mentor and former fellow workaholic, Wayne Cotton. Cotton went seven years without a single break. That led to seven legal judgments, eight stress-related health issues, and a near seven-figure mountain of debt. When he finally unplugged, his health improved—and his businesses' revenue doubled. (Already a seven-figure earner, nobody was more shocked than Cotton himself.)

Cotton has since developed a color-coded calendar system that forces one to slow down thanks to one color in particular, yellow. Mellow Yellow time (or "M.Y." time) is time scheduled to unplug or deload. It's personal time dedicated to relaxation, hobbies, and activities unrelated to work.

When you see me in Whitefish, Montana, I'm on Mellow Yellow time, recharging. I encourage you to schedule Mellow Yellow time quarterly. Since 2020, I've recommitted to doing the same. (You can learn more about Wayne's color-coded calendar system, and Mellow Yellow Time, at CottonSystems.com.)

Mind

Listen to Lin-Manuel

Lin-Manuel Miranda conceived of his groundbreaking Broadway musical, *Hamilton*, while on vacation. "It's no accident that the best idea I've ever had in my life—perhaps the best one I'll ever have in my life—came to me on vacation," he revealed. "The moment my brain got a moment's rest, *Hamilton* walked into it."

Elite intellectuals, like elite athletes, sprint and rest. Bill Gates, co-founder of Microsoft, takes annual "Think Weeks," during which he isolates himself in a cabin to think, rather than do. Employees who take more vacation days report higher levels of productivity, morale, and motivation than those who take fewer days off. Plus, "neuroscience proves that the 'aha' moment comes when you're in a relaxed state of mind," says Pulitzer Prize-winning journalist Brigid Schulte. That's why your best ideas appear on a walk, in the shower, or on vacation. Good things come, or "walk," into your life when you slow down.

Soul

The Parable of the Overworked Farmer

In a fertile valley lived a farmer whose dedication to his crops was unmatched. Believing that ceaseless work was the key to unparalleled harvests, he toiled from dawn until dusk, never pausing, never resting. Meanwhile, his neighbors embraced the rhythm of the seasons, working diligently but also taking time to rest, repair their tools, and nourish the soil.

As the seasons turned, the farmer noticed, to his dismay, that his yields were diminishing, his soil turning barren from overuse, and his once-sturdy tools breaking under the strain. In contrast, his neighbors' fields bloomed abundantly, their tools lasted longer, and their health and spirits were high.

2

Gratitude – Bad Knees, Full Heart

Early December 2020

I didn't listen to the whispers. My friend Tony Dungy didn't listen to the naysayers.

On January 22, 1996, Dungy's pedigree as an NFL player landed him the top job as the head coach of the Tampa Bay Buccaneers. At the time, the Bucs were the laughingstock of the league. The team had suffered double-digit losses nine of the previous 10 years. They hadn't had a winning season in a whopping 13 years. Nobody gave 31-year-old Dungy a chance. He was too inexperienced. Too unproven. Too young.

Too young... Is that how I should feel now, today, as I hobble down a hospital hallway gripping a walker? Mere months before my 50th birthday?

I had my right knee replaced in 2018, at just 48 years old. A physical sign, a manifestation, that I was beginning to crumble. Yet, that was before the pandemic. Before the closures. The emptiness. The furloughs. The deaths. The death threat. And so on. And so forth.

Then, as if punishment for not listening to the whispers, for not slowing down, it happened: My left knee gave out. The pain started in July of 2020, just weeks after *Get Your Mind Right* came out. I was too busy to really feel it. I was attempting to save the gym. To save the community. To save my world. My second wind masked my pain.

Now I was paying for it. Your body keeps score. And the cartilage in my left knee was lost. It was gone. Rigid bone was scraping directly on rigid bone. You can imagine the pain. When December rolled around, I couldn't help but feel the pain.

Two major surgeries in two years for the fitness guy. Talk about an identity crisis. I couldn't work out. I could barely move. Who has two knee replacements by age 50? This guy. Yikes!

I look like a senior citizen, I thought, while draped in a billowing hospital gown... again. My posture was bent, just far enough for me to observe the pulsing whites of my knuckles gripping the rubber handles of the walker. I couldn't walk without it. It felt like I was gripping those metal bars for dear life.

What is happening to me? I wondered.

As I inched my way down the hospital hallway, the nurse to my left cheered me on: "Look who's walking!" she said—like a coach, encouraging a player. My, oh my, how the roles had reversed. I was, obviously, no longer a player. But now, was I even a coach? How could I coach, inspire, impact, from a walker? Ugh. Her Buccaneer-red scrubs make me think of Dungy.

There was little to cheer for during the Bucs' first year with Dungy at the helm. His naysayers were right. The team's losing ways continued. The Bucs began his first season with five straight losses, 0-5. They finished a putrid 6-10. Dungy expected to be slid a pink slip that off-season. But it never came.

In turn, Dungy flipped the script his second year. His Bucs went 10-6. A miraculous turnaround. By the next season, his third, the Bucs were Super Bowl contenders. Just two seasons later, the Bucs were division champs. The team accomplished the impossible: Earning playoff bids in Dungy's fourth, fifth, and sixth seasons. Get this: Dungy had already won more games than any other coach in franchise history by the end of his sixth season. Yet, that's when his dreaded pink slip appeared. Dungy was inexplicably fired just 48 hours after leading the team to their third-straight playoff appearance.

Word spread late at night, just hours after a team spokesman declared Dungy's status wouldn't be determined until the coach met with the owners, the Glazers, the following day. No wonder his players were ticked. Wouldn't you be? Dungy transformed the Bucs from perennial cellar-dwellers to perennial playoff contenders in record time. As one journalist stated, "He raised the dead."

"Unfair," Buccaneers punter Mark Royals grumbled. "A disappointment," Pro Bowl safety John Lynch bellowed. "I'm at a loss for words," cornerback Ronde Barber croaked. Dungy, himself, appeared ticked, too. The newspaper, the primary form of media back then, quoted him as saying the following shortly after learning his fate: "It's my understanding that they're going to have a press conference [this morning at 10:30] so I'll do my talking at the press conference."

Oh boy. Buckle up, baby.

My understanding is Dungy was locked out of the team's facility the night before the press conference. Security had to usher him in to gather his belongings. My guess is security ushered him in for the following day's press conference too. What would Dungy say? What might Dungy do? What would you do? What would you say?

Tony Dungy said thanks. Literally.

He thanked the team. The players. The fans. Even the owners, the Glazers, who fired him amid a historic run (and had reportedly made their decision to let him go long before Dungy was ever made aware). He even tapped a media member on the shoulder to thank them for the kind words they'd written about his mother, Cleomae, who had passed away during the season.

"I wanted to be bitter… but I couldn't. I was hurt, disappointed, but I also wanted to thank the Glazer family for giving me the job," Dungy later recounted. "I was fired from here but I was also hired here. I was hired when I had never been a head coach—no one else gave me a chance."

Tony Dungy didn't just insist on attending a press conference, *the* press conference, to announce his very own firing, he took the podium for one reason and one reason only: To express his gratitude. Unbelievable.

Another journalist added, of Dungy, "There he was, in the very depths, to the very end, stopping to thank someone."

Man, that stuck to me like glue. Life felt unfair at times. I was hurt. I dealt with disappointment. Heck, I even felt betrayed. At the time of my second knee surgery, in December 2020, I'd discovered a team member or two had leveraged Fitness Quest 10's tough times to plot competing gyms down the street. I can't even begin to tell you how much that crushed me. I wanted to be bitter. Plenty of times, throughout 2020, I was at a complete loss for words.

Yet, trudging along that hospital hallway, looking down at the steel bar of a walker, I found myself feeling incredibly grateful. "Thank you" flowed out of my mouth like a river. I high-fived the red scrubs-clad nurse beside me. Why? Because despite another knee surgery, a second replacement, I was grateful for my left knee. Heck, it lasted longer than my right. My left knee gave me nearly 50 good years!

You may know of my football career. I was a Division I quarterback at William & Mary. I even played quarterback professionally, in NFL France. But before all that, I was a standout soccer player. And an all-conference kicker and punter in high school (as well as being named an All-Shore Quarterback). My point is, my knees had been used and abused for decades—soccer, football, training, STRONG, you name it.

Yes—the pain was bad. And surgery was the pits. But the emotional anguish was perhaps worse than the physical. Because, for me, "recovery" meant weeks on end with no coaching. No training. No working out... again. Fitness Quest 10's doors had just reopened, yet I was locked up at home. Imagine that.

But boy did my *right* knee feel good. It felt brand new, too. It *was* brand new. That first replacement, in 2018, was worth it. In all likelihood, my left knee would soon feel good as new. And when it did, I bet it could easily give me 50 more years. This second knee surgery, though not ideal, suggested my body would finally be right. And that made my mind right. After all, we can complain because rose bushes have thorns. Or rejoice because thorns have roses.

Now it's not lost on me how easy it is to say, "Be grateful." And how easy, even naturally, gratitude flows like a river during good times. But what about during bad times?

I often compare gratitude to a muscle. It strengthens with proper training. Thank God, in the years and decades that led up to that first and then second knee surgery, I'd gotten my reps in.

You see, back in 2014, I began sharing bite-sized motivational messages every Monday—videos, audios, notes, and quotes—called a "Dose of Durkin." My kids literally grew up on those "Doses." Forget D.O.D.—we even had a D.O.B.—a Dose of Brady (my youngest son Brady) one week. My daughter, McKenna, and my eldest, Luke, made plenty of appearances in weekly Doses, too. As did our fur baby, our beloved golden retriever, Jersey. Jersey made his inaugural appearance at just 8 weeks old. Hundreds of Doses were shared with tens of thousands, if not hundreds of thousands of people, around the world. But my favorite ones, the messages that stand out most, tend to be the ones shared every Thanksgiving, in which my family and I listed off the many things we were grateful for that year, including each other.

Over time, a "Dose" evolved into a "DOSE." An acronym for Dopamine, Oxytocin, Serotonin, and Endorphins. The "feel-good chemicals" or "happiness chemicals" that our brain releases when we exercise. Guess what? Science shows gratitude releases a literal DOSE, too. Gratitude can change the molecular structure of your brain. Said differently, gratitude is as physical as it is mental. It's also an activity, not just a thought (or afterthought).

The paradox of gratitude is that the more grateful we are, the more reasons we find to be grateful. Gratitude begets gratitude, creating an upward spiral of positive emotions and experiences. As renowned brain coach Jim Kwik says, "What you appreciate, appreciates." Think about that.

If the nurse beside me had slid my walker aside and led me to a podium, my message would have echoed Dungy's: Thank you.

Thank you. Thank you. A new knee has been bestowed upon me. And soon, I will be back on my feet and better than ever.

Guess what else I was secretly thankful for? A sabbatical. Albeit a forced one. Was it exactly how I imagined it? A knife to my (other) knee? Draped in a hospital gown? Creeping around on a walker? Of course not. These weren't my wilderness years... or months. I wasn't whistling from the mountaintops in Whitefish, Montana, like I so desperately wanted to. Instead, I was fresh off a gurney, hobbling home to sink into my off-white La-Z-Boy recliner... finally forced to slow down.

The truth is, I was grateful for the break. In a way, I was grateful for the surgery itself, as it provided a "forced sabbatical." I would never have taken time off if my body hadn't demanded it. And the timing, in some ways, couldn't have been better. Not only did I desperately need to unplug, or deload, but the pandemic was also showing signs of easing up, too. After three years of unprecedented stress, soul-searching, exhaustion, fatigue, burn-out, pain, worry, uncertainty, and so on and so forth, I looked up from that walker and thought to myself, *Things are finally looking up!*

Body
Walk It Out

In a podcast interview with Jon Gordon, the *New York Times* bestselling author of *The Energy Bus,* Jon told me that "you can't be stressed and thankful at the same time." Then he took it one step further: He shared that he regularly goes on "walks of gratitude." While there are plenty of expected and obvious ways to strengthen your gratitude muscle—writing hand-written notes, sending texts, and journaling to name just a few—consider a walk of gratitude. (Turns out *The Energy Bus,* Jon's most illustrious book, the vision, the story, all of it, came to him... on a gratitude walk.) Walk it out, baby. Today.

And as you walk, think about the things, people, and situations you are grateful for. This practice can transform a regular, mundane activity into a powerful exercise in mindfulness and positivity, shifting focus from what's lacking to what's abundant in one's life. Plus, by walking, by moving, you'll release a DOSE in more ways than one.

Mind

See Gratitude

When you struggle to *feel* it, *see* it! One of my favorite components of my home office is my "gratitude wall." I pin reminders like photos, pictures, even hand-written letters, from trainers, coaches, listeners, followers, interns, employees, Masterminders, even readers to it. Nowadays, I even print emails, then pin them to my gratitude wall to serve as visual reminders of all the things I have to be grateful for. (After all, I started this practice back in the days of snail mail.)

The "wall" is no more than a corkboard. Yours can be the same. Or you can use your fridge. A file folder. A computer folder. You name it, to collect—and save—reminders of gratitude. In fact, the notes I referenced in the Introduction from Adam Ferreri and Tyler have both been placed on my Gratitude Wall.

Soul

The Cherokee Fable of the Two Wolves

An old Cherokee tells his grandson about a battle between two wolves inside him. One wolf represents negativity, anger, and bitterness, while the other represents positivity, peace, and gratitude.

The grandson asks, "Which wolf will win?"

The old Cherokee replies, "The one you feed."

3

Growth – My "Moment of Release"

Late December 2020

The most scared I had ever been was when I opened the doors to Fitness Quest 10. I was 29 years old. Single. Solo. I had no clients. No money. No business plan.

Therefore, I had nothing to lose.

(My best friend, the late, great Ken "Sawman" Sawyer made that abundantly clear to me: "You have nothing to lose, literally!" he squealed as he slapped his knee.)

Not anymore.

As 2021 quickly approached, I'd almost lost Fitness Quest 10 to a global pandemic. I'd been through the ringer with loans, laws, furloughs, finances, frustration, burn-out, betrayal, and physical pain that, of course, led to multiple life-pausing surgeries. I couldn't let Fitness Quest 10 go. I wouldn't let it go. I refused to pull the plug. Like I said, "I'll go down before the ship does."

Yet, now, after weathering several storms, and with a heckuva lot to lose—my home, my family, and all the things I didn't have back when I flung open the gym doors in 2000—I was craving change. Massive change. Again.

You see, prior to the pandemic, in 2017, I first heard that whisper. "Yoo-hoo." But when the pandemic flipped my world upside down, *our* worlds upside down, I tuned it out. Now, on the other side of the coronavirus chaos, with Fitness Quest 10's doors reopened, that whisper returned as a shout, as if mad that it had been muted.

And that whisper wasn't just calling for change. It was a call... *for change.*

Something was stirring. In my gut. In my soul. I was seemingly successful on the outside, yet I was feeling unfulfilled on the inside. I was searching. Searching for something more. Something different. Something even greater. *Yeah, greater.* I needed to experience, or accomplish, something greater. I needed to step into something deeper. And I knew I had it in me to do it. But I didn't know what "it" was.

That tug for change, that ongoing call from God, pulled me way back to 2003. That's when LaDainian Tomlinson first caught wind of my work with one of his San Diego Chargers teammates and requested to train with me in the off-season. I, excitedly, told him to give me a call after the season.

When any professional sport season concludes, the majority of athletes escape. Winners collect a check, celebrate with a parade, fly first-class to the Magic Kingdom—"I'm going to Disneyland!"—and have the red carpet rolled out for them at the White House.

The rest? They get rest. A break. Time with friends and family. A vacation somewhere exotic. Or, just a chance to be home, present, for more than a day or two. The 2003 NFL regular season

Growth – My "Moment of Release"

concluded on a Sunday. Less than 24 hours later, early that Monday, LaDainian Tomlinson called: "Todd, I'm ready," he said. And sure enough, on Tuesday morning, LaDainian stood outside the doors of Fitness Quest 10. Come to think of it, he looked like he was ready to run right through the doors. He was intent on training, right then and there. No rest needed.

That was the norm for the next several off-seasons. Until it wasn't. After winning the League's most illustrious individual award in 2006, the MVP, LaDainian again appeared at the doors of Fitness Quest 10. But this time, he wasn't as intent on training. Instead, he asked if we could talk. Then he asked just one burning question:

"What's next, Todd?"

"Uhh... what do you mean what's next, Dain?"

To me, it was incredibly obvious. Staring him in the face. "We run it back, baby!"

Run it back?

LaDainian looked at me disappointed, confused, even defeated. He seemed surprised that I didn't understand what he was actually asking—that after years of training in the trenches, spending every off-season together, I couldn't read between the proverbial lines—and that I spit back such an obvious answer.

LaDainian didn't want to "run it back." And for the life of me, I couldn't understand why. He was at the top of his game. Heck, he was at the top of *the* game. Why would we change anything, even a single thing, now?

Yet, there he was, craving a change. Massive change. Craving something... different.

Between you and me, I stewed on that conversation, LaDainian's question, my response, and his reaction, for years. I was truly baffled by it. Until December of 2020. Some fourteen years later. Because guess what? I was craving change, too. I wanted something more. Something... different.

By 2020, I'd enjoyed several crests, several years of success: Fitness Quest 10 had collected numerous awards and accolades. And post-pandemic, in what was called the "new normal," it was more of the same: The gym was humming along again. I'd built an A-list client list that stuck with me through thick and thin. I, too, had won the fitness industry's MVP award, Personal Trainer of the Year, twice. And shortly before the pandemic, I was inducted into what I consider the fitness industry's Hall of Fame when I earned the coveted Jack Lalanne Award. Plus, I told myself, my stint on *STRONG* wasn't *that* long ago.

But I didn't want to "run it back," either.

The idea of things returning to how they were before the pandemic didn't light me up like it used to. I was burned-out. Completely burned-out. I didn't have the juice. The "energia." I wanted more. But not more of the same. I didn't want to "run it back" because I didn't want the third quarter of my life to be the same as the second. I didn't want my next 25 years to look like my previous 25.

Plus, I couldn't shake that whisper—that "yoo-hoo." By late 2020, I was hearing it, feeling it, almost daily. Like a pebble in my shoe, it wouldn't go away. As it grew louder, it became clearer: I was being called *away* from Fitness Quest 10.

How can I change the world, expand my impact, when I'm working around the clock as owner and operator? When I'm constantly putting out fires? Creating new programs? Trying to keep everyone happy? Solving people problems?

Growth – My "Moment of Release"

I sensed I may soon feel almost resentful of my gym, even resentful of the thing I loved most at my gym... the people. I was tired, drained, from running 'round the hamster wheel. That wheel, that shell, was Fitness Quest 10. Yes—I was safe inside. But I was also stuck. I was protected, yet exhausted. And nearing age 50, I realized, for the first time ever, how confused, and even unfulfilled I was. Man, that realization hit me like a ton of bricks. Tony Robbins' words began to rattle in my head: "Success without fulfillment is the ultimate failure."

I almost lost Fitness Quest 10 during the pandemic—now I was being called to... leave it?

What a "mind screw." Crazy thoughts swirled in my head daily: *Was I a failure? The ultimate failure? Can I really leave my "baby?" Or at least a portion of it?*

There's no place like home... and Fitness Quest 10 was home. It was my Magic Kingdom. Over the past 20 years, I'd spent exponentially more time inside those four walls than I did anywhere else—including my primary residence. Yet that whisper, that calling, was telling me, shouting at me, to step away. If I was to create a more prolific impact, reach my 10 million, do more, do greater, and ultimately quell that restless stirring in my soul, I needed to bust out of the proverbial hamster wheel.

But boy was I petrified. The problem was I didn't know what was on the other side, other than the unknown. I knew I was stuck, but what was I searching for? What if this was just some sort of veiled mid-life crisis? What if a cherry red Corvette was the actual answer? What if stepping away, abandoning the business I built, was actually a massive mistake? What if that whisper was like a long game of telephone, and I was now hearing the wrong, convoluted message? If I stepped away from Fitness

Quest 10, what was next for me? I had no idea. And at 50 years old, the unknown is far scarier than at say 19, or 29, years old. (If only "Sawman" could see me now, I thought, with clients, with money, and with a business, though no plan.)

As I was searching for what was next, so was my teammate, Jeff Bristol. Jeff and I met in 2014 during his interview for a front desk position at Fitness Quest 10. An interview Jeff aced from the moment he shook my hand. Jeff radiated remarkable energy, pure joy, and genuine sincerity. He was a young buck—I'm almost 20 years his senior—who had that "it" factor, that aura that I always look for. I remember thinking, *Where did this guy come from?*

Jeff grew up in nearby Temecula, California. He came from a loving family. He was the oldest of three. A sharp kid. And a stud athlete—an All-American wrestler who earned a Division I scholarship. You could tell by looking at him. He checked every box, a budding superstar who would fit Fitness Quest 10 like a glove.

The only thing that could have stopped me from hiring Jeff back in 2014 was a background check. Good thing we didn't do them then, because Jeff had a record far longer than his resume.

Sadly, Jeff spent the majority of his 20s in two places: Jail and rehab. While his college friends were starting families and careers, Jeff was abusing drugs. Overdosing was not out of the ordinary. No parent wants to outlive their child, yet Jeff's parents were forced to imagine his funeral. There was a point in time that Jeff's problem grew so severe, his mom and dad spent tens of thousands of dollars in repeated attempts to save him. (They'd do anything for their son—wouldn't you?)

One year into his Fitness Quest 10 tenure, in 2015, unbeknownst to me, Jeff relapsed. Sam, his wife, had temporarily

Growth – My "Moment of Release"

moved cross country, to New York, to pursue her master's degree. She flew home to San Diego for the holidays and caught Jeff red-handed, using. By that time, Jeff had been sober for one full year, basically since joining Fitness Quest 10. He slipped back into bad habits in just one month without Sam.

Sam rang me to share the tragic news. And to inquire about Jeff's future at Fitness Quest 10. My heart sank for Jeff, for Sam, and for their families. Sam expressed how badly Jeff wanted to keep the job, how important it was *for* him and *to* him. I was admittedly torn on what to do. I loved the guy. But you normally don't get a second chance after using at the workplace; it's too risky, for everyone involved.

But I believe in second chances. I always have. So following a come-to-Jesus conversation and his signature on a behavioral contract, which included random drug screenings, I made the decision to hold Jeff's front desk job at Fitness Quest 10. It would give him something stable to return to after completing rehab. That was one of the most difficult decisions I made in the history of Fitness Quest 10. It also proved to be one of my best.

And over time, Jeff was elevated from his original role. Hopping from lily pad to lily pad as I like to call them. He was great at the front desk. Even better when he came out from behind it—shadowing our world-class personal trainers on the fitness floor, with his sights set on becoming one of them. Then he did. In fact, Jeff became our busiest personal trainer. *The* busiest personal trainer at one of America's Top 10 Gyms.

When I first heard that "yoo-hoo," that whisper, to do more, I began to give Jeff Bristol more. More responsibility at Fitness Quest 10, so I could step away more and more. First, I elevated Jeff to assistant general manager. No surprise, he crushed it.

And then to the top spot at Fitness Quest 10, general manager. Again, Jeff thrived.

But elevating Jeff, even to general manager, didn't allow me to step far enough away from Fitness Quest 10 to do something more or greater. To uncover what was next. To find "it." As Jeff was jumping from lily pad to lily pad, so was I. But now I was being called to a whole new, mystery pond. And to get there, I needed to *leap*.

And to leap, I'd also need to let go. That whisper was demanding it.

I've often compared my headspace in late December of 2020, years after burn-out initially struck, months after the death threat, weeks after my second knee surgery, and days after the COVID-related closures finally felt fully behind us, to being consumed by the uneasy feeling an unseasoned trapeze artist faces at the "moment of release." In his book *Warriors of the Heart*, author Danaan Perry shares "the parable of the trapeze": "Every once in a while as I'm merrily (or even not-so-merrily) swinging along, I look out ahead of me into the distance and what do I see? I see another trapeze bar swinging toward me. It's empty and I know, in that place in me that knows, that this new trapeze bar has my name on it. It is my next step, my growth, my aliveness calling out to me. In my heart of hearts I know that, for me to grow, I must release my grip on the present, I must let go of the well-known bar, and leap to the new, unknown bar."

Bingo. That was me.

I was swinging on one safe, steady, familiar bar—Fitness Quest 10. I had been for almost 21 years. And now, letting go was what I was wrestling with. I'd been pushing off, or brushing off, that "moment of release" since 2017. My second wind during the pandemic? That was just a pseudo-wind. Until I finally let go, I'd be stuck, not-so-merrily swinging, just "running it back" at Fitness Quest 10. And ignoring the whispers.

I feared that heart-stopping moment of release, being suspended between bars, after both hands let go. Because I'd have to let go of most everything I knew, everything that was safe and familiar. And then, for what? What's next? I still didn't know where I was going. Or where I wanted to go. Thus, the thought of being suspended between worlds made my mind race with a thousand doubts, a thousand what-ifs.

What if I mistimed the release? What if now is not the right time? What if I simply can't do this? What if I'm not strong enough? Brave enough? Good enough? Young enough?

Ah, but once you've seen that proverbial bar swinging towards you, or in my case, heard that call, it's impossible to "unsee" the bar, as it continues to call. Yep—I was facing a "trapeze moment." My trapeze moment. My moment of release. And to get unstuck, I needed to let go.

When LaDainian Tomlinson requested to train with me in 2003, he asked only one question: "Can you get me to the next level?" That was his version of running a background check. And my answer was, "Sure thing, LaDainian." Because I believe there's always another level.

It's a phenomenon that's been studied by psychologists like Dr. Carol Dweck, who coined the term "growth mindset." Dr. Dweck argues that our ability to embrace challenges and take risks is directly related to our belief in our own potential for growth and change. In other words, the trapeze artist who can let go of the bar is the one who believes, deep down, that they have the ability to reach the other side.

I believe I have that ability. For the record, I believe you do, too. We all do.

That's why, just three weeks after my second knee surgery, I did it. *I let go.* I sold the majority of Fitness Quest 10—maintaining a small piece for my soul—to Jeff Bristol. Now I could get out of the day-to-day. Ironically, I took the leap from my La-Z-Boy recliner—still searching, but no longer stuck. Wondering what would be next, but knowing it would be different, bigger, and even greater... once I got back on my feet.

I was still scared, but excited. Exhilarated, even. The thrill of something different, of honoring that call, the adrenaline of making a big decision, of rolling the dice, well, it lit me up. It fueled my growth mindset. Plus, the timing was darn near perfect. A new year was just unfolding. Between the burn-out, the death threat, the closures, and the surgery, 2020 was hands down the worst year of my life. The deepest valley. But 2021, well, instead of running it back, I was starting fresh! And that lit me up.

On top of that, I was just weeks away from being back on my feet, floating into 2021 with a fresh bionic knee, ready to leap into a new pond. As I looked up at the TV from my La-Z-Boy, I thought to myself, *things are (finally) looking up again. 2021 is going to be a BIG year. Let's go, baby!*

Growth – My "Moment of Release"

Body

Release Your "Anchor"

Every December, for the past 15 years, I excitedly clear several days to complete my "Annual Strategic Roadmap & Life Plan," now simply known as my "God-Sized Dreams Planner." It's perhaps the best of my best practices, a journal curated with 80+ questions inviting one to reflect on the past year, plan the next year, and design their future. From personal experience, I've found that when you go deep to answer the illuminating questions inside, this practice doesn't just shape your year—it shapes your life. It's like magic. So, I encourage you to grab a pen and answer the following question plucked from the 2024 version of my "God-Sized Dreams Planner."

Question #64: Letting Go of Your "Anchor"

What is "it" that you NEED to let go of (personally, professionally, relationally, financially, etc.) that's holding you down or back?

Mind

The Paradox of Safety

The safer you try to be, the more you risk. This paradox encapsulates the trapeze artist's dilemma—clinging to the bar, they're safe, yet only by releasing it can they achieve the spectacular, risking the fall to grasp something beyond. This mirrors life's paradox, where too much safety can stagnate growth, and risk is often the pathway to significant achievement.

The Roman philosopher Lucius Annaeus Seneca said, "It is not because things are difficult that we do not dare; it is because we do not dare that they are difficult." Famed poet T.S. Eliot observed, "Only those who will risk going too far can possibly find out how far one can go."

I often equate this paradox to playing prevent defense on the football field. You're not playing to win—you're playing not to lose. It's a strategy that, while intended to secure a win by minimizing risk, often leads to unexpected and unwelcome losses. You won't win the game of life playing prevent defense.

Soul

The Monkey and the Coconut

Picture this: A monkey comes across a coconut with a small hole in it, just big enough for the monkey to slip its hand inside. When the monkey reaches in and grabs a fistful of the sweet coconut meat, it finds that its hand is now too large to fit back through the hole. The monkey is faced with a choice: Let go of the coconut meat and free its hand, or cling to its prize with its hand trapped inside the coconut.

The coconut represents the familiar, the comfortable, the known. It's the job we've held for years, the relationship we've settled into, the habits and routines that define our daily lives. For me, it was Fitness Quest 10. Like the monkey, we often cling to these things out of fear or comfort or complacency. We're afraid of what might happen if we let go, but our refusal to let go is often what holds us back from reaching our full potential. We become so focused on holding onto what we have that we lose sight of what we might become.

4

Perspective – My Back and "The Conversation"

February – March 2021

"Forget my knee," I groaned to my physical therapist, Martin. "My *back* is killing me." I assumed it was just a flare-up. So did he. We couldn't have been more wrong.

Just six weeks after knee surgery, and a few weeks after selling Fitness Quest 10, I was in the hospital… again. Stuck, again. I'd decided after stepping away from Fitness Quest 10, I would step further out into the world, filling my 2021 schedule with keynotes, so I could spread more impact, and reach my 10 million. My knee was almost fully healed, and I was just gearing up to hit the road, when my back suddenly started bothering me.

Now I'm no stranger to back pain. Fitness Quest 10 was born following the journey of healing my own back—sans surgery. After college graduation, I played professional football in Southern France, as a quarterback in the NFL Europe League (like a developmental league for the NFL). During one game in March of 1996, I rolled right of the pocket, tucked the ball, and sprinted forward. Once I crossed the first down line, and secured a fresh set of downs, I slid to safety. I slid to avoid getting hit.

And then: BAM! I got hit. A pair of linebackers crushed me at full speed in my most vulnerable position. Their helmets crushed my back. Motionless, disoriented, I "came to" on my back. My trainers and teammates looked down at me, as I looked blankly up at the pale blue sky. When the feeling in my legs slowly returned, I was gingerly guided off the field on a gurney. Then shot up with painkillers. Somehow, I played the next game. In fact, I played well.

Then the painkillers wore off. And, well, despite my fair share of pains, strains, sprains, and concussions from decades absorbing hits on the gridiron, I'd never felt agony like that before. I needed help walking to the bathroom. Picking up a fork. Getting to the hospital. Even lowering myself onto the exam table. Then an X-ray revealed I'd need to pursue a new dream, as becoming an NFL quarterback was officially a pipe dream.

The diagnosis was three herniated discs. Spinal stenosis. And degenerative back disease—at just 25 years old. The topper: I could barely lift my left foot; it dragged on the ground, like an anchor. That "drop foot" or "slap foot" suggested a potential neurological issue. No wonder I felt darn-near paralyzed. The prognosis? Surgery. A 90% chance of it.

Armed with Vicodin to numb the pain, I traveled to 13 cities over three years, showing my back to every healer, guru, bodyworker, light worker, massage therapist, chiropractor, Reiki master, you name it, in a relentless attempt to dodge surgery. And guess what? I did. I dodged surgery. By the end of 1999, my back pain was gone. And I was moving on to my next dream: Opening Fitness Quest 10.

Perspective – My Back and "The Conversation"

Melanie says we should have known. She's probably right. With two knee surgeries in the books, over just two years, something had to give in 2021. During each knee surgery, the medical team killed two birds with one stone. When they exchanged each worn-down knee bone for fresh metal, they also addressed my severe bowleggedness: Realigning my hip, knee, and ankle to straighten each leg. In 2018, they corrected the nine degrees of curvature in my right knee. Two years later, in 2020, they tackled the seven degrees of curvature in my left knee.

It made perfect sense biomechanically. Until it didn't. Like I said, something had to give. Guess what gave? My back. Straightening my legs, which had been compensating for my spinal issues for years, was probably the final nail in the coffin that brought my old back injury back to life years later. The very thing that helped bring relief to my knees had unintentionally triggered a new wave of pain in my back.

Are you kidding me?

I had just let go of the trapeze. I made the freakin' leap. Faced my fears. Faced my "moment of release." Why? So I could bust out of the four walls of Fitness Quest 10 and spread even more impact. Now, just as I'd scraped myself off of my La-Z-Boy, and was finally feeling physically able to hit the road and step up onto the stage, excruciating back pain that I hadn't felt in 25 years decided to rear its ugly head again.

What the far is going on? I thought to myself.

"Let's get it looked at," Melanie suggested. So we did, on our 20th wedding anniversary.

Then after the familiar chirp of an X-ray, I heard the tech mutter something under his breath: *"What the f*ck?"*

I rushed over, behind the partition, as quickly as my back would allow me to. Then I caught a glimpse of what was troubling him. Once I saw it, I couldn't unsee it. (My guess is you won't be able to either.)

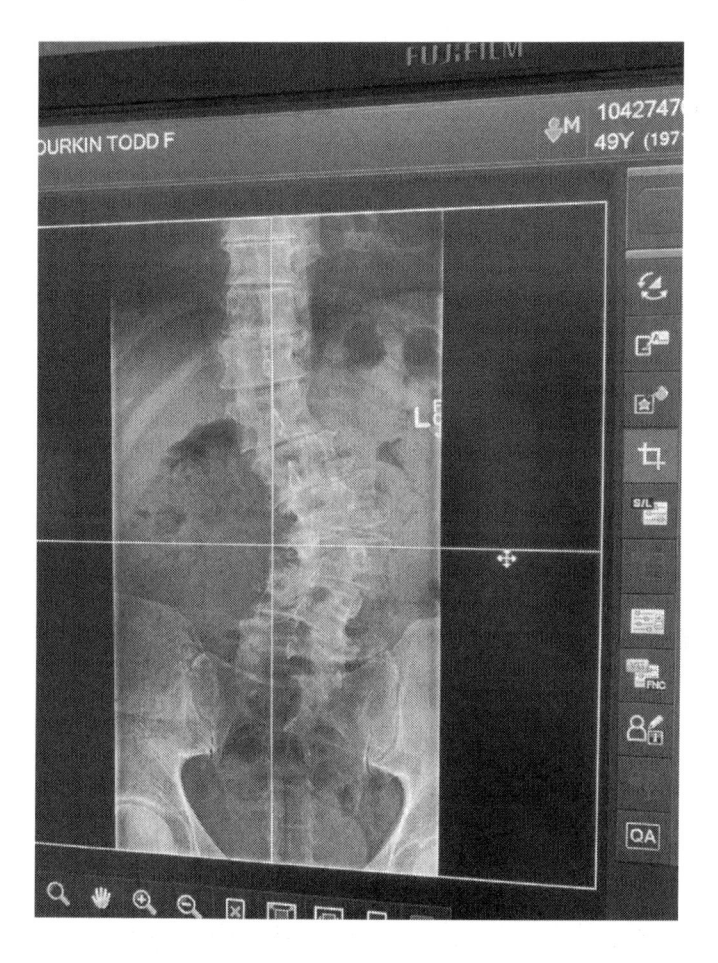

"Is that MY back?" I asked the tech, pointing to that gruesome image lighting up the X-ray machine's monitor.

"The doctor…," he stammered back, "will call you… as soon as possible." The tech hurried out of the room. Then, sure enough, my phone buzzed what felt like seconds later.

Perspective – My Back and "The Conversation"

"Todd, did you serve in Afghanistan?"

"No, doc…"

"Iraq?"

"Nope."

A long, perplexing pause followed. "It looks like… a grenade exploded in your back," he said. "How are you doing what you're doing, Todd? How are you even walking?"

Heh. You tell me, Doc.

He went on to detail the stark absence of space, "none," in my lumbar spine. "Your discs have disintegrated," he said with a hint of fatigue. "All of them." This meant the discs—the cushions, those pliable pillows nestled between each vertebral bone of my spine—had vanished. Picture that scenario: 33 hard bones relentlessly grinding against each other, up and down my warped spine.

Hence the exacerbated curve. A slight curve is relatively common. It's called scoliosis. But as you near a 20-degree curvature, doctors consider bracing the spine. My curve was near-double that. My spine had a gruesome 39-degree curve. And at 39 degrees, as the doctor explained, even a back brace would never be enough. With such an alarming curvature, the body contorts, organs are compressed as if squeezed by an unseen fist, breaths are drawn shallow, and nearly every movement is shadowed by pain. Yes, every movement. The lungs and the heart are squeezed into a space that's just not designed for them. It's like stuffing a large balloon into a small box. You can blow it up, but it won't expand. Therefore, every time you even take a deep breath, it can feel like you're only getting half the air you should. Therefore, my pain, or relative lack thereof, was what really struck him. To him, it was a near medical miracle that I was walking under my own power. And in that moment, as he shared how I should be feeling, my pain escalated. Suddenly, I hurt as bad as my X-ray looked. Maybe even worse.

"It's time to see the back deformity specialist," my doctor advised. "He handles cases like these. I can't help you with a back like this."

The back deformity specialist? That's a thing? Yikes!

I couldn't get on the back deformity specialist's schedule for a full month. Later that day, Melanie and I flew to Sedona, Arizona. Hours later, my back pain was so bad, I had to be carted across the parking lot from the hotel to our rental car. Worst anniversary trip ever.

I continued to feel helpless day after day, week after week, like I was stuck in some sort of torture chamber. The pain that flooded my body wasn't going anywhere—only growing worse. Simple tasks, like tying my shoes or reaching up to a shelf, became a painful reminder of my "condition." After seeing the contortion, I was now *feeling* the contortion. I felt twisted. Knotted. Broken. Beaten. Deformed. Even disabled. That X-ray was ingrained in my head.

Meanwhile, I wrestled into a back brace every morning. Since I wasn't speaking on stages, I was training a few select clients to keep myself sane. They exercised. I didn't. I couldn't. Yet, I heard the murmurs around me: "Look at TD! He's fired up today! Let's go, baby!" You see, the one and only position I could occasionally unlock a moment of relief in was the one position they'd seen me directing clients from for years: Crouching in the universal coaching stance. Legs wide. Knees bent. Back angled (just right). My stance had them fooled, so did my energy. I was relying on

Perspective – My Back and "The Conversation"

caffeine to spark me up. In doing so, I had everyone fooled; they had no idea what I was suffering through.

<hr>

After enduring a month or so of this relentless daily torture, the long-awaited day of my appointment with the back deformity specialist arrived. Upon entering the room, his nurse paused. She looked down at her clipboard, then back up at me.

"Todd… Durkin?" she asked, tilting her head to the side, and scrunching her nose toward her brow.

"Yep… that's me."

I could see confusion in her eyes. She wasn't baffled by my back—she was baffled by *me*. I was not the usual clientele at this clinic. Apparently, she was expecting a crippled, 90-year-old man, perhaps in a wheelchair, or at the very least, gripping a walker. At 50 years old, I was decades too young to be there. Decades too young to see the back deformity specialist for any kind of legitimate reason. And as a former athlete, and lifelong fitness trainer, I was seemingly too physically fit to be there, too. I'm sure she thought it must be a misdiagnosis, or some kind of mistake.

Then the doctor entered the room. He shook my hand, then clipped my X-ray to the nearby lightbox. "This might be the worst back I've ever seen," he said earnestly. *Great. My back is the worst back the back deformity specialist has ever seen.* What a strange feeling; it felt like I was winning an award—one I never wanted to be nominated for, let alone win.

And then, for the first time in more than a month, on that day, in that clinic, there was suddenly one thing—and one thing only—as bad as the tentacles of pain shooting up and down my spine, neck, and legs: His proposed solution. A two-day, 14-hour surgery where he'd cut right into my back to reconstruct my spine. (I darn near blacked out as I pictured the region from my mid-back to my tailbone folded open like a book cover, a team of doctors looking down upon my winding spine with screws, rods, chisels, and saws in hand.) This surgery was so intense, so complicated, it came with a chance of disability... and even death. "You may be permanently disabled," the doctor cautioned. Either way, "Your life will never be the same." Ugh. Plus, the recovery period was as extreme as the surgery. "You'll need to take an entire year off," he added.

My eyes closed. My head sank into my hands. I was in complete disbelief. I'm not sure I'd still fully bought into the X-ray. Maybe it was a cruel joke. Photoshopped. Altered. Though, my pain indicated differently.

When I'd sold Fitness Quest 10 a few months prior, I was searching for something different. But a different surgery, more surgery, was not what I had in mind. *How did I go from a death threat to what felt like a potential death sentence in less than a year? What did I do to deserve this? Yet, how could I not go through with surgery?* I had two options: Live with this unbearable pain... or survive the complicated surgery, then 365 days of being stuck to the La-Z-Boy, unable to move, let alone exercise. *Darned if you do, darned if you don't*, I thought.

So what do I do?

I thought about my wife, Melanie, whose hand I was gripping. I thought about the burden I could become to her. I thought about my kids: Luke, McKenna, Brady. What would they think of disabled Dad? I thought about the burden I could become to each of them. I thought about my clients. What would they think? As well as my social media followers and fans. My "Mind

Perspective – My Back and "The Conversation"

Right Maniacs." They couldn't see me like this. I thought about the gym, Fitness Quest 10. *Was letting go a mistake? Was I being punished for my growth mindset? Was reconstructive back surgery really what was "next" for me? Is this what the whispers wanted?*

I believe it was Melanie who compared my prognosis to that of a healthy person getting diagnosed with cancer. I guess I felt like I couldn't catch a break. Remember, the whispers started after *STRONG* aired. The burn-out began to balloon shortly after. It knocked me off my feet in 2018, forcing me to have my knee replaced to stop the pulsating physical pain. Then the pandemic hit. It shuttered our doors for much of 2020. It skyrocketed my stress. Financially. Mentally. Emotionally. Then BAM: My other knee gave out in 2020. The good one. I was knocked off my feet again. I felt crippled, again. My soul-searching hit a painful crescendo. I sold the majority of Fitness Quest 10 shortly after. I left my baby in search of something more, something different, something even greater in December of 2020. And now, months later, this is what I get? That prognosis was the straw that broke the camel's back.

My mind spun as I stared down at the ground during the short, lumbering walk from the clinic to the car. Melanie was talking to me, but I didn't hear a word she said. I was just trying to keep myself somewhat composed, to maintain what now felt like a façade of pseudo-strength, until we settled into the car.

When we did, the dam broke. A tidal wave of pent-up tears poured down my cheeks. My voice reduced to a whimper as I turned to Melanie and unloaded question after question. I was questioning everything.

"Who am I? What am I? What the heck is going on? How is this even possible? What am I going to say? What am I going to do? What are they going to say? What are they going to do? Where did I go wrong? What did I do to deserve this?"

I was quaking with fear, anger, frustration, and confusion. At this point, I couldn't "run it back" even if I wanted to. I couldn't afford to take a year off—mentally, physically, emotionally, or financially. I'd just sold my business. I listened to the whispers. I filled my schedule with keynotes that, apparently, I wouldn't be able to attend. I'd be glued to the freakin' La-Z-Boy for what would feel like an eternity. Unable to walk. Unable to move. Unable to dream. Unable to think. Unable to do... *anything*.

I continued to spiral. "Why me, Melanie? And why now? I'm supposed to help all these people. I'm supposed to impact 10 million lives. I'm the get your mind right guy... Mr. Mind Right Maniac! And now... how can I help anyone if I can't even help myself?"

I don't remember every question I continued to rattle off, but I remember the rest all started with the same word: "WHY! WHY! WHY!"... until Melanie interrupted.

"Stop... Stop... Stooooop, Todd!" Her eyes held mine. "Stop feeling sorry for yourself!"

Then she unloaded her questions: "Have you ever considered that the 10 million people you've been aiming to impact aren't the ones God has in mind for you? That maybe this is all happening *for* you and not *to* you? What if 10 million is just the beginning? What if it could be 100 million? Maybe He brought you to this point for a reason... maybe there's another plan at work. Maybe this is part of God's plan. Maybe God has a plan for you to impact more than just fitness professionals, and clients, and

Perspective – My Back and "The Conversation"

members of Fitness Quest 10. Where is your faith, Todd? Maybe now is the time that God is going to do His deepest work on you. Maybe it's time to listen..."

"What about MY plan, Mel!? What about me?" I snapped back.

"Maybe it's not about you, Todd...," she said slowly, deliberately, through clenched teeth. "He will carry you. He's got this. Now is the time to do what you have been preaching all along... it's time to TRUST Him even more."

Though I continued to cry, I heard her—loud and clear. Her perspective had power. For years, from every stage, every social media platform, and beyond, I'd pronounced to hundreds of thousands of people things like, "Your future must be bigger than your past", "Your dreams must be bigger than your memories", and "The devil wouldn't be attacking you if there wasn't something valuable inside of you." After all, as Dr. J says, "Thieves don't break into empty houses."

Maybe I needed a dose of my own medicine. Maybe Melanie was prescribing it, forcing me to take it. But I didn't want to. Not then. Not at that moment. It was all too fresh for me. I didn't want to hear it, not from her, not from anyone. I kept crying, and questioning. But truth be told, she was right. And deep down, I knew it. I just didn't know if I had inside of me what it was going to take to walk through it.

Everybody has something: Drew Brees' mom died by suicide six months before he led the Saints on that epic 2010 Super Bowl run. Hal Elrod wrote his bestselling book, *The Miracle Morning*, following a car accident that left him clinically dead for six minutes (and a cancer diagnosis, on top of it). J.K. Rowling's dementors were inspired by her real-life battle with depression.

My good friend, Mike Merrigan, was walking down a sidewalk in 2019 when he was smacked by a car traveling 50 miles per hour. It was life or limb, literally. He chose life. Doctors proceeded to amputate his left leg. I then penned these words to Mike: *"Mike, it's a Sunday morning. And I'm sitting here pondering what happened. We've been praying for you. And I can't stop thinking about you. Mike, as much as I want to say I'm sorry. I can't. And I won't. I want to say from the bottom of my heart, I love you. And congratulations! God's chosen you, Mike, to a calling way beyond what you could imagine. To a purpose way deeper than you could have ever envisioned. Mike, your story and your life just got ordained. Remember... to whom much is given, much is required. You've been given a great new gift, Mike. The requirements just became greater. Never forget that. Brother, it's time for massive IMPACT! We've got a world to change. – Love, Todd & Family"*. "Congratulations" is probably not what Mike expected to hear. Yet, it must have been what he needed to hear: Mike later told me he looked at that letter every single day in the hospital.

Melanie challenging me to 10x my dream amid agonizing back pain was not what I expected to hear. My first back injury was my "something" nearly 25 years ago. Healing it trained me, qualified me, and led me to opening Fitness Quest 10. Was my back my thing... again? Now? 25 years later?

Maybe my back was happening *for* me, not *to* me. Or maybe not. Maybe I was just unlucky. Paying for dodging surgery I should have had nearly 25 years ago. And ponying up for speeding up, when for years, I should have been slowing down.

At the end of each weekly episode of *STRONG*, two teams, each made up of a trainer like me and their trainee, would go

Perspective – My Back and "The Conversation"

head-to-head in a series of intense physical challenges inside a daunting physical structure—a four-story monolith inspired by American Ninja Warrior—dubbed the "Elimination Tower." The Elimination Tower was purpose-built to chew us up and spit us out—when I say us, that included me and the nine other world-class trainers, many of whom were former professional athletes, and all of whom were younger than me. That weekly showdown determined which of the two teams on the chopping block would be eliminated and which would continue in the contest. Winners stay. Losers go home… and lose their shot at the grand prize of $500,000.

Nobody wanted to go into the Elimination Tower. Except me. On national TV, I gave the Elimination Tower my own name: The "Opportunity Tower." I attribute that perspective to why I survived it more than every other trainer on the show. Elimination? No. Opportunity? Yes. That was my perspective. In the car, at that moment, I needed Melanie's perspective.

Melanie closed our conversation with a tender, "I believe in you, Todd. I love you and we will get through this TOGETHER. But God is the quarterback in this one… not you."

She wasn't calling me out, she was calling me *up*. What if this setback was actually my set-*up*? For "it?" For that thing? That something more? That something different? That something bigger? That something even greater? On the drive home following that life-altering appointment with the back deformity specialist and that subsequent conversation with Melanie, I remembered the late, great Wayne Dyer's wise words echoing in my ears: "Change the way you look at things… and the things you look at change."

Body
Leap The Line

When my friend Mike Merrigan lost his leg, I remember wrestling with the following questions in the immediate aftermath: What can we do? What can I do? What would you do? I did two things:

1. I wrote the aforementioned letter to Mike. It was long. Deep. That's why I wrote it on a poster board that his brother hung for him in his hospital room. On the other side, was the second thing I, or *we*, did for Mike.

2. On the flip side of that poster board, I wrote the words "MIKE CAN" in massive block lettering. Beneath those two words, my family, and our Fitness Quest 10 family, each wrote something Mike could still do, to remind him of who he was, and to give him our... perspective. It said things like: Mike can laugh. Mike can hug. Mike can live a life worth telling a story about. Mike can... drink beer. (The former owner of a San Diego-area bar, Mike got a kick out of that one.)

Perspective – My Back and "The Conversation"

In our personal valleys, we all wrestle with similar emotions. And we all could benefit from a little perspective. Here's some for you: Don't dwell on what you can no longer do. Focus on what you *can* do. Stuck in the vice grip of that excruciating back pain, guess what I could do? I could write. I could pray. I could reflect. I could meditate. Eventually Amber Kivett and Dr. Mike DeBord of B3 Sciences introduced me to BFR (Blood Flow Resistance) band training. BFR bands were instrumental in my healing—and my mindset—because they allowed me to exercise again.
What about you?

Draw a vertical line down a sheet of paper. On the left side, you can if you so choose, acknowledge the things you can't do. Then leap over the line. Head to the right side of it. And write down all the things you can do. Then, you guessed it, start doing them.

Mind

"Benefit Finding"

Look around the room, right now, for anything brown. Scan your surroundings for just five quick seconds or so. Now close your eyes and tell me everything you noticed that was *red*.

Good luck. You saw a lot more brown than red, didn't you? Why? Because you were looking for brown. Try again. Look around the room, right now, for anything *red*. Now close your eyes and tell me everything you saw that was red. You found more red this time, didn't you? Of course you did. *Because you were looking for it.*

Once you develop a belief, you find what supports it. You will even find stuff that's not there to support it. You'll call something beige that's actually brown. Or something burgundy that's clearly red. If you think you're messed up, you're going to find things that support this belief. You're going to, in some ways, "color" yourself that way. Whatever you believe is self-evident. Tony Robbins proved this by sharing this exact exercise with comedian Theo Von. I hope it has the same impact on you as it did on Von. Remember, when you look for the benefits, or the blessings, you will find them.
(Watch the video here:
https://www.youtube.com/shorts/iqVKSF93sME)

Perspective – My Back and "The Conversation"

Soul

There Must Be a Pony in Here

According to a popular parable, in a small, picturesque town lived twin boys. One was shadowed by pessimism, the other brimmed with optimism. Their differing perspectives became the talk of the town, so much so that a local psychologist decided to conduct a simple yet revealing experiment.

The psychologist invited the pessimistic boy to a room in his office: The room was filled from floor to ceiling with the latest toys, games, and books. The boy frowned. He stood there, surrounded by every child's dream, yet he worried aloud about the toys breaking, the games eventually boring him, and the dread of having to tidy up.

The optimistic boy was led to a different room. One filled entirely with horse manure. The boy's eyes lit up with excitement. Without hesitation, he jumped in and started digging fervently. The psychologist asked the boy what he hoped to find amidst the manure. Beaming with joy and without stopping his search, the boy replied, "With all this manure, there must be a pony in here somewhere!"

5

Stillness – "The Letters"

April 2021

For Frida Kahlo, it was painting. She poured her pain onto the canvas. For Beethoven, it was music. The thrill of sailing put wind in Einstein's sails. Emily Dickinson was a baker. Elizabeth Gilbert, a gardener. For Jiro Ono, it's preparing sushi. For Andy Puddicombe, the co-founder of Headspace, it's juggling. (Yes, juggling.)

For me, it's writing. It's been that way since middle school. Heading into eighth grade, I was nominated as a Pop Warner All-American Scholar Athlete. To be one of the just 50 nationwide nominees-turned-winners, I'd have to translate my prowess on the football field to prose. I'd have to write several essays to win the judges over. I was just 13 years old at the time, still a full year away from even stepping foot in high school. I had about as much experience writing as I did juggling—in essence, none.

Luckily, my dad had plenty. He was a prolific writer in his spare time. I remember regularly spotting yellow legal pads—covered with pages of cursive words I could barely make out—strewn around my childhood home. From the ping pong table in our basement, my literary training grounds, Dad educated me on the importance of a strong opener, "a hook!", as he handed me my very first journal, an empty yellow legal pad to outline those essays upon.

Then he crouched down, looked me square in the eyes, and the coaching commenced: "It's third and 15," he barked. "The crowd is loud!" He slowly turned his head to the left, and then the right. "Durkin walks up to the line of scrimmage and gazes out over the defense." His brows lifted. "He can see it: Not just the first down, but the game-winning play that is about to unfold." His voice grew more excited. He stood tall. "Today is Durkin's day. It's touchdown time. It's his time!" BAM! Hook, line, and sinker. Dad had me. He sold me, then and there, on the incredible power of the right "hook." And introduced me to the thrill of writing.

The coaching continued: "You'll need a strong close, too," he stressed. "Only after you make your points." And then, after a long, thoughtful pause, he said, "And more importantly, most importantly... let the pen flow, son."

Flow, it did.

With Dad's help, my essays helped earn me that All-American award. And from then on, I kept writing. So did Dad. Years later, while I was attending college at William & Mary in Williamsburg, Virginia, Dad wrote to me every single day. Like clockwork, every afternoon, there'd be a fresh, handwritten letter from Dad waiting at the campus post office for me to excitedly retrieve. Until there wasn't.

I received the devastating news on February 18, 1992: Dad had suffered a heart attack. I immediately flew home from Virginia to New Jersey. I saw him in the hospital that night. It was

Stillness – "The Letters"

the last time I ever saw him. My father passed away on February 19, 1992.

For 20 years, he was my best friend. My biggest fan. My most caring coach. My top mentor. He was that person we all have. That one person I couldn't lose. And I lost him. The following morning, he was... gone.

Forget college—I embarked on a cathartic farewell tour, visiting the places where I shared my most fond memories with Dad—the inlet at Point Pleasant, the football stadium at Brick High School, the Great Auditorium in Ocean Grove—and cried. And cried. And cried some more. School was an afterthought. So was football (even though I was supposed to be competing for the starting job at the time). Then after three weeks of misery, I heard a whisper. "Yoo-hoo." I *swear* it was Dad. And that whisper, *his* whisper, encouraged me to go back to school.

Back on campus, I mustered up the courage to visit the post office, knowing my mailbox would be empty. Except it wasn't. There was an envelope inside. Dated February 18th, 1992.

I couldn't believe it. It was another letter from Dad! He licked the stamp the same day he had his heart attack... and just one day before he died. I tore the envelope open, right then and there, with tears of joy rolling down my face. You see, Dad seemed healthy at the time of his heart attack. His death was a shock. There was no time to mentally prepare. One day he was here. Seemingly healthy. The next, he was gone. But, maybe, just maybe, Dad knew he was running out of time...

"Life is very precious," he wrote. "It's all about time, Todd. Be sure to use it wisely." He listed the things I might become in time. Now a football player. And a student. Later, a teacher, a doctor, a coach, a lawyer, a speaker. Perhaps, even, an author. He signed off with this: "I will always love you regardless of WHAT you do. It's WHO you become that's most important and the TIME you spend with those you love. I love you son, Dad."

Yes—Dad must have known he was running out of time. Now, nearly 30 years after receiving Dad's last letter, I asked myself: *Am I running out of time?* Though unlikely, I'd been warned the nature of my surgery could kill me. Meanwhile, the daily pain I was battling was robbing me of living any kind of normal life. More, the mental and emotional pain of feeling deformed, crippled, crushed, broken, it was all dragging me down, into a dark, dark place.

I had a 10% chance of skirting major surgery in France back in the 90s. And I did it. Could I accomplish the near-impossible again, in 2021? I wouldn't go down, under the knife, without a fight. I couldn't stomach a year off, no matter how much pain I was in. So on my mission to feel alive again, to overcome that hideous X-ray and escape my seemingly inescapable pain without reconstructing my deteriorating spine, and "living" my third quarter of life from a La-Z-Boy, I found myself in Tijuana, Mexico. Tucked inside a hyperbaric chamber. A long metal tube plucked from a sci-fi movie for hyperbaric oxygen therapy.

Stepping into a hyperbaric chamber is like stepping into a spaceship. The door seals, then the chamber is gradually pressurized with pure oxygen. I felt a slight popping in my ears, similar to what you experience during takeoff in an airplane. But from then on, the only thing I heard was the slight hum of the machinery working to maintain the pressure.

Space. Silence. Stillness. The perfect environment to write. To escape. In that moment, writing became my escape. I was armed with my instruments of victory: A pen and my brown, leather-bound journal. Then I heard a whisper: "Let it flow, Todd. Let it flow."

Flow, it did. From my parents' ping pong table to that hyperbaric chamber, I've always found writing, or journaling, to be like a science-backed "cheat code" for life. As famed Stanford neuroscientist Andrew Huberman revealed, writing promotes proven improvements to physical and mental health—particularly when focused on stressful and traumatic events. And in that silence, I had my fair share of stress to write about.

I felt myself enter that intoxicating flow state. Breathing, thinking, writing. Listening for more whispers in a cocoon of near-silence and stillness. That narrow chamber made me feel like I was almost back in the womb—a safe, sacred place. Performing an ancient practice—writing—inside a cutting-edge contraption.

※

The following is "the letter" I wrote to myself on April 30, 2021— from a hyperbaric chamber in Tijuana, Mexico. (I never stopped journaling during this time. As a matter of fact, I wrote and journaled more than ever before.)

April 30, 2021

In a hyperbaric chamber in a Medical Clinic in Tijuana, Mexico.

Here I sit in a hyperbaric chamber in Mexico contemplating life. It's an 8' x 15' submarine-like chamber with two beds and a chair. Former UFC World Champion Dominick Cruz is lying on a bed to my left and Brendan Loughnane, an up-and-coming UFC fighter is lying on the bed to my right.

We came down here together to treat our ailments; mine far worse than my younger counterparts.

I'm sitting on a chair, as the guys relax, watching "Rocky" on a small 15" inch TV. Could it be a sign?

This hyperbaric chamber is our first "treatment" in a day that will be full of them, to hopefully help my back and find some answers.

We'll do an IV drip complete with NAD+, plus electrolytes and other vitamins and minerals. I'll also have a consult with a doctor regarding the viability of stem. What he says, as well as the cost ($10,000?), will help determine the next step for my back.

Man, my back. I don't know what to say, other than how did I get here? Not only to Mexico, but this entire situation. I've been in agonizing, life-altering back pain for months now.
It's debilitating. My entire life has changed.

I think: What is it telling me? Why am I here? How did it get this bad? Is this permanent? How can I go back to feeling good again? Or how can I at least get out of this pulverizing pain that is dominating my life?

I knew it was bad... I just didn't know how bad it really was. At this point, 6 doctors or so have confirmed its severity. And the bad news keeps coming.

Stillness – "The Letters"

I have some big decisions to make. Really big decisions. For example: Surgery? When?

And it's not just "surgery." It's the most intensive, invasive back surgery one could possibly have. So bad that only a back deformity specialist can do this surgery.

It's a full-blown fusion. 3 rods. All the way from T12 to S1. 20 screws.

There's a 39° curvature of my spine. Major disc degeneration. There is no space between my discs and there are many potential problems looming.

Great. I really did it this time.

I don't want surgery.

Why is God handing me this problem... and why now?

It makes no sense to me when I look at the last several months. First, Covid. Shutting down the business. Furloughing 42 people. Opening and closing. Inside and outside.

Then knee replacement surgery.

Then a business transaction with Jeff, intended to allow me to finally do what I feel my next decade is all about... speaking, writing, coaching, mentoring, creating content, and a whole lot of IMPACT.

Then 6-weeks into knee rehab... BOOM! My back. It started to hurt. And then it got worse and worse and worse. I finally got an x-ray on our wedding anniversary. I saw it. Scary. I heard the results. Even scarier.

The doctor said, "How the heck are you doing what you're doing? This is the worst back I've ever seen." WOW!

I couldn't believe it. I knew the road ahead was going to be a long one... and I didn't know where it was taking me.

Sleepless nights. Fatigue. Exhaustion. Feeling of being lost. Empty. Burn-out. Depressed. It all consumed me.

I navigated the medical system over several months. Many experts were perplexed that I am not even in more pain than I am now. One concluded our visit with this: "I hate to say this, but the doctor can't help you. This is beyond his scope."

I interrupted her... "But I thought he was the back specialist surgeon."

She said, "He is. But he can't help you. There is only one person who can help this and he's a Back DEFORMITY Specialist."

Next thing I knew, Melanie and I are sitting in the Back Deformity Specialist's office. "Wow. This is one of the worst I've seen," he said.

This is not what I had signed up for, I thought. I just sold the majority of my business so that I can go out and conquer the world. I wanted to do new things. Podcast. More speaking. More books. Help even more people. Create even more impact.

And here I was facing a "Death sentence." OK, maybe it's not a death sentence, but it sure feels like one.

More questions flooded my head.
How long will it take me to truly heal and before I can do my first talk?
Can I do a Mastermind retreat or event 10 weeks after the surgery?
When can I go for a walk around the block again with my wife and Jersey again and be free?
When can I start training again at a level that I want? I'm talking about lunges, step ups, bench press, and lying on my back. Is it 8-weeks? Is it 16-weeks? Is it 32-weeks?

Will I ever get back to normal? Can I ever get back to living my dreams?
So many questions... and so little answers.

Stillness – "The Letters"

The next doctor I talked to was running an hour late. I was livid. I wanted to rip him a new one. Instead, I handed him my most recent book. A signed copy of "Get Your Mind Right."

I said, "Doc, you don't know me well yet, but I'm not your average patient. I'm on a mission to motivate 10 million Americans to get their mind right and I'm gonna need you to be on my team if I'm gonna fulfill my mission."

He stopped me. He apologized for being late and said, "Tell me more about your goals. This is interesting."

"Doc, I'm 50 years old and I got 60 more good years left. I'm living to 110. But I think I'm gonna need a new back. And I need you to be my guy. Can you help me with that?"

He proceeded to tell me step by step ALL that was going to happen.

And then he said it's time to schedule surgery. He brought out what looked like a "book" of papers to sign. And I just couldn't do it yet. I just couldn't sign my life away because of what it said in those documents and the risks of such a dangerous surgery.

I told him I would need to pray about it before signing.

I left the office and went into my car and cried like a baby to Melanie. Never had I cried like this before in front of her. What I said to her scared me. And what she said to me was so what I needed to hear. She is one of the very few people who knows just how bad it has gotten and how scared I am of doing what is ultimately inevitable.

I hope I get answers today...

Back in 2007, I wrote several intentions on a notecard. One of which was to land a sponsor. An apparel sponsor, for Fitness Quest 10—the facility, team, and me. What felt like days later, I met the late Bill Hampton on the sidelines of a practice field, where he was scouting football players to potentially sign. Bill worked for Under Armour. I pitched him on sponsoring us. Under Armour was just a budding brand then, trying to compete with the Nikes of the world, so Bill was open to the unorthodox idea of sponsoring the people training the athletes and the facility where the athletes trained (not just the athletes themselves). He told me to whip up a proposal.

I handed Bill a three-inch-thick stack of papers the following day. When he asked me how long I worked on that proposal, I told him, "My entire life." He laughed. I didn't. I never told him that I stayed up the entire night writing that proposal. Nor did he know that just six months earlier I had set an intention on a notecard that came true when I signed with Under Armour days after Bill read my proposal. My point? Writing always pays off for me—in one way or another. Whether I dream of something good, or am experiencing something bad, I write. Cathartic. Therapeutic. Call it what you want.

On that day, in that hyperbaric chamber, writing gave me an opportunity to make sense of the nonsense. I poured my fear, uncertainty, unknowingness, frustration, pain, confusion, all of it, onto the pages of that brown, leather-bound journal. Letting the pen flow, upon page after page. In fact, I wrote down another intention then and there: "I'll do anything" to avoid surgery, to dodge a full, incomprehensible year off. And I meant it. I made the decision at that moment: *Anything but surgery.*

Stillness – "The Letters"

I scooted out of the hyperbaric chamber feeling refreshed. Relieved. Even, dare I say it, a bit of physical relief. Maybe it was the oxygen. Maybe it was the stillness. Maybe it was both. Soon after, the medical team at that mud-slab clinic known for their array of treatments that could help heal even the most jacked-up professional athletes broke the silence to share some unfortunate news: There's "nothing more we can do for you," they informed me. Even stem cells, a cure-all of sorts, weren't "viable" for my situation.

My spine must have been listening. Pain, once again, flooded my body.

Body
The Most Difficult Exercise You Can Do

"All of humanity's problems," Blaise Pascal wrote in 1654, "stem from man's inability to sit quietly in a room alone." Man or woman, silence is the hardest exercise anyone can do. It's the hardest exercise I do. Finding comfort in the quiet is... uncomfortable. Especially in a world where we are conditioned to be busy. This world where we're always on and never off. Isn't it funny: The most difficult exercise we can do is simply being still.

For me, silence is built into my "3-2-1" nighttime routine. Three hours before bed, I have my last meal. Two hours before bed, I start winding down. I stop working. I focus on family. One hour before bed is when the magic happens. I shut down. This is when I amp-up my self-care. No TV. No phone. I pause. I quiet the mind. Many nights, I journal in silence. That's just me. Most importantly, I listen. I reflect. Sometimes, I meditate. The bottom line is, I sink into the silence. The stillness. What about you? Try it *tonight*. It doesn't have to be one hour—make it a minute, or three, or five, or 10. Ready... 3... 2... 1.... GO!!

Mind

The Neuroscience of Silence

In silence, we find the loudest growth. This paradox suggests that in moments of quiet and rest, away from the hustle and distractions, we experience the most significant personal and professional growth, as these moments allow for reflection, learning, and rejuvenation.

I know this to be true. And science proves it to be true: The World Health Organization links "noise pollution," or excessive noise, to significant health concerns. Meanwhile, silence can develop new cells in the hippocampus (Kirste et al. 2013), a key brain region associated with learning, memory, and emotion. And another study (Arsland, 2017) found that the ability to tolerate silence is associated with greater physical resilience and better mental health outcomes.

Soul

The Sound of One Hand Clapping

Longing to unlock the secrets of the universe, a young monk approached a wise Zen master. Sensing the young monk's eagerness, the master decided to test his understanding with a question: "What is the sound of one hand clapping?" the master asked the monk. The monk's brow furrowed. He began to ponder the question. The more he thought, the more elusive the answer seemed. Days turned into nights, as he was consumed by his quest to understand. Finally, he went back to the master and asked, "How can it be that a single hand can clap and make a sound?" The master smiled. "It can't be heard," he said. "It is something that can only be experienced."

The monk bowed to the master and left. He continued to meditate on the question. But this time, he did not try to understand with his mind. He simply let go of all thoughts and allowed himself to be. One day, while he was meditating, the monk had a sudden realization. He smiled. He finally understood the sound of one hand clapping. It was not a sound at all. It was the sound of silence.

In this context, this kōan, or paradoxical Zen riddle intended to challenge conventional thinking, can be seen as an invitation to explore the space between thoughts, the quiet that underlies all sound and activity. When we clap with two hands, we create a sound that fills the air. But when we hold one hand still, we create a space for silence to emerge. It's a reminder that in silence, one can find answers that noise cannot reveal.

6

Hope – A Hotel in Mexico and Breaking the Cycle

June – September 2021

There's always another level.

Just as my pain would settle in at a 7, 8, or 9, it'd jump to a new level. Off the charts at times. Many times.

And that was despite my abnormally high pain threshold. (Remember, based on pain alone, I originally thought I was dealing with a flare-up, not a tortured spine.) Who knows how long I'd managed to tune out the pain? But now, I was paying for it. My entire body was getting blasted day after day, week after week, month after month, as I attempted to skirt surgery.

Though the pain wasn't going away, I still wasn't willing to go under the knife. Not yet anyway. Unstoppable force, meet immovable object. Despite my best efforts, the pain was truly unstoppable. Literally and figuratively. But a two-day, 14-hour surgery that would shelve me for a full 365 days was not an option. Since I'd dodged back surgery once before, my stubborn DNA suggested I might be able to do it once again, perhaps choosing to forget that when I avoided surgery the first time, I was 25 years younger and in my physical prime.

Following my diagnosis in early 2021, I embarked on a several months-long voyage exploring a range of modalities, in multiple clinics, countries, and disciplines, in a frustrating effort to knock my pain down even just one notch. In the Bahamas, I underwent cutting-edge stem cell therapy, hoping to regenerate damaged tissues. Countless steroid and cortisone injections punctured my skin, too. I surrendered my body to a carousel of skilled massage therapists, each technique promising a unique path to healing—from Swedish to Shiatsu, no stone was left unturned. I tried Egoscue therapy to realign my posture. ELDOA techniques to restore mobility to my rigid joints. Hyperbaric oxygen therapy, as well. I did as much breathwork as I did bodywork. And the list goes on and on. Courtesy of my client list, I had lots of options. But even the stuff typically reserved for big shots with big pockets didn't offer much relief.

Then in June 2021, after months of physical torture, I trekked back to Mexico. This time to Cabo San Lucas for my eldest son, Luke's, senior trip after his high school graduation. I knew traveling would be risky for my back, but my heart won the battle with my head thanks to some coaxing from Melanie. We agreed to make it a short trip—a compromise, given my condition.

In the wee hours of the morning on day two of our trip, at 2:36 a.m., my pain reached a new level: I was wrestled awake as if the sharp blade of a samurai sword had been stuck directly into the most fragile part of my lower back.

I couldn't walk, so I crawled. Army crawled. From the foot of the bed, across the carpet, and into the tile-floored bathroom. Miraculously, I eventually made it to the toilet and mustered up just enough energy to fling my arms around the bowl. Then came the vomit. Lots of it. It wasn't Montezuma's revenge—it was the pain-killing pills, the sleeping pills, all of the pills I'd been taking to manage my agony. I hung over the toilet, like a 20-something who had several too many, with my chin grazing the seat. My head felt heavy, near-impossible to lift, probably because it was now an extension of my writhing spine.

What's next? Tears. Lots of them. The pain. The pressure. Then the pleading. "Melanie, I need something, anything, to numb the pain," I said. "I'll try anything." And I meant it. Curled up in a ball on that cold, hard floor, my hands clutching my knees, I begged Melanie to hunt down painkillers, drugs, whatever Mexico had to offer. She refused. "Call an ambulance, then. Let's go to the E.R. I'll do the surgery," I said.

"Not in Mexico," she replied.

My back was broken, literally. I was broken, too. That exact word, "Broken," was penned in my journal countless times. My body was so compressed and deformed I'd shrunk two full inches. And to top it all off, I hadn't gotten even one good night's sleep in several months, if not longer.

On the bathroom floor, Melanie held me. Embraced me. Like a mother holds a child. We attempted to numb the pain with love. And when that didn't work, prayer. I prayed for stronger painkillers. She prayed we could make it back to the States. Her prayer was answered. We made it back the next day, but I was an absolute mess. Physically and mentally—I'd reached a new low.

And over the next several months, things didn't get any better.

I couldn't lie on my back. Or on my stomach. On a rare, lucky night, I could catch two, maybe three hours of sleep, from one precise position: On my left side. Tucked into the fetal position.

With a pillow scrunched between my bionic knees. Even then, I still needed at least a serving size of sleeping medications and the stars to align to catch much shut-eye. Pillows felt like cinder blocks. Sheets felt like sandpaper.

In the mirror, I gazed upon a stranger. Was this the *Get Your Mind Right* guy? I looked tired. Old. Beaten. Broken. I could see the pain in my blue eyes. New grey forming in my hair every day. The soul had been sucked from my face, like I'd been in a stare-off with one of Rowling's dementors.

My beloved dog, Jersey, looked at me like I was a stranger, too. Disappointment filled his eyes as our morning walks became a thing of the past. "Sorry, Jers," I'd grumble. I'd fall into the chair, or the couch, as he rushed over with his leash hanging from his mouth. I could almost hear him begging, "Just one time around the block, Dad, c'mon! No? Fine. How about the mailbox? Please, please, puhleeeease." But I couldn't even make it to the end of the driveway without wincing in pain.

During the majority of 2021, the rigid structure of that hidden back brace was the only thing that kept me upright, on my feet. And even that failed at times. My spine was so compressed, so mangled, I felt like I couldn't do anything. For months, I was just a shell of myself, refusing to tell anyone for fear of "becoming my back." If you've been in physical pain before, you know what I mean—if you give your pain a voice, it can easily become the only topic of conversation and thus, impossible to escape. I refused to let that happen.

Then August came. Two months after my breakdown in Cabo San Lucas, it was time to send Luke off to college. Talk about bittersweet. It was exciting for him. Heartbreaking for Melanie and me.

I played quarterback at William & Mary. Now Luke, too, was set to be a college quarterback. Like father, like son. Only he'd be attending Davidson College in North Carolina, 2,400 miles away from our home base in California. For the first time in our lives, after 18 years of sharing a hallway, an entire country would be between me and my oldest son.

Somehow, I staggered on the plane, and survived the five-hour flight from San Diego to North Carolina. Yet, despite being in the same state and city, I missed the heart of that ceremonious trip to see our eldest go off on his own.

After arriving in North Carolina the previous day, I couldn't get out of bed on the big move-in day. Heck, I couldn't move. I guess the five-hour flight, secured to a cramped, uncomfortable seat, caught up to me. While the rest of the parents were helping their sons and daughters move in, settle in, and get acclimated, I was cooped up in a dark hotel room, glued to a bed in excruciating pain, just steps from campus.

It pains me to say this, but the next day, I had to literally apologize to my son during our tearful, final embrace, our last hug before I staggered back on the plane, and he was officially on his own as a college student. The guilt I felt boarding that plane pointed back to California was almost as unbearable as the paralyzing pain that prevented me from being there for my son on that once-in-a-lifetime move-in day. I felt like a loser father. Despite my high pain threshold, I couldn't crawl out of bed, let alone experience those final bonding moments with my son: The Target runs, the orientations, the campus tours, you name it.

I continued to feel like a prisoner in my own body, held captive by pain while life's precious moments slipped through my fingers. And thus, the problem. The pain was always there. Yet it was still unpredictable. And it always seemed to hit the hardest, reaching a new level of intensity, at the most inopportune times.

Before, during, and after Luke's sendoff, I shuffled into what felt like dozens of different offices and clinics, seeking just one "second opinion" that offered an alternate path out of pain. I was pleading for good news, temporary relief, or, in some sort of alternate universe, both.

I got the opposite.

One medical professional waltzed in and shoved a nine-centimeter needle in my back, without so much as a "hello." That cold, deflating experience made me feel less than human. Like cattle. Or even a cadaver. Plus, if anything, that shot only made the pain worse.

Then there was the surgeon who did lots of talking. Too much. He shared how thrilled, excited, he was to potentially operate on me as he rubbed his hands together like some sort of mad scientist. You could hear the giddiness, the delight, in his voice as he admired my mangled X-ray then promised me a "J-Lo booty" as a bonus of operating on my "virgin" back. All while running his fingernails, disturbingly, up and down my backside.

What universe am I in now?

I felt worse *leaving* many of these offices and clinics than I did going in. I also felt the scales tipping; I wondered if the risks of operating on my back still outweighed the risk of my body, my health, even my mind, deteriorating any further.

I finally, begrudgingly, spoke of waving the white flag here in the States. Somehow, we'd find a way to clear the calendar for an entire year. We'd make ends meet during that time. Even if my life would never be the same, I should, at the very least, experience some relief—if only while knocked out and numbed up under the knife.

But then, at the 11th hour, in August 2021, everything changed: I found the right clinic, the right nurse, the right radiologist. A caring nurse rested her tender hand on my back. I could *feel* her silent prayer. She knew of the world of pain I was in, and how long I'd been trapped in it. While she kept her palm resting on me, the radiologist gently slid the point of an epidural into my skin. And guess what… he hit the "sweet spot." That needle worked like magic—it felt euphoric.

I've always believed in the healing power of touch. It's no coincidence that my thesis at San Diego State University was titled "Physiological & Psychological Effects of Massage Therapy and Touch on Stress & Anxiety." That nurse's tender hand amplified the physical relief of that amazing epidural, but it also gave me critical emotional and psychological support during one of my most vulnerable moments.

Finally, after more than half a year of enduring relentless back pain, I felt human again. As I rose from the exam table, the nurse looked into my tear-stained eyes and offered a smile I'll never forget. Though we'd never met before, in that moment, I felt a deep connection to her—a shared understanding. I knew what she was about. And I have a feeling she knew what I was about, too.

I didn't just leave that clinic relieved, I left with a warm, compassionate hug… and a ton of newfound *hope*. I felt like skipping out of there. Maybe I'd even bust a move, moonwalk to the car. But as thrilled as I was to experience relief in that moment, I also knew the truth: That shot was probably just a temporary solution to a lasting, and much larger, problem, like a band-aid on a bullet wound.

Though surgery still loomed, that appointment gave me a jolt of hope I hadn't felt in a long, long time. Just enough hope to follow through on seeing *another* back deformity specialist, before making the call to schedule surgery. It seemed my experience with that radiologist and nurse began to break the vicious cycle I was trapped in, a cycle I call the "pain-fear loop."

In 2009, I released an educational video series called "Optimal Performance Bodywork," or OPB for short. The four-disc DVD bundle revealed my take on fascia, lengthening, and bodywork, much of which was learned first-hand, following my first brush with back surgery. (Surprise: Before I was a personal trainer, I was a bodyworker. And before I trained LaDainian Tomlinson, I was a sports massage therapist for the San Diego Chargers.)

Optimal Performance Bodywork DVDs

The pain-fear loop is as simple as it sounds: Pain leads to fear. And fear leads to pain. It's not just a loop, it's a cycle. More pain leads to more fear. More fear leads to more pain. One feeding into the other. And I'd been stuck in that loop, that vicious cycle, since my initial diagnosis. Since that horrific X-ray that revealed a grenade, of some sort, had exploded in my back, directly on my spinal cord. How do you break the cycle? How do you hop off that merry-go-round of pain and fear? With one thing: Hope. I taught it then. I was living it now. I was breaking free from the cycle.

When a person has hope and believes that a treatment will work, their brain releases neurotransmitters like dopamine and endorphins that can lead to a reduction in pain perception and an increased sense of well-being. A DOSE. On top of that, research has shown that hope can influence the body's physiological responses to pain. For instance, one study showed that patients with chronic pain who underwent a hope-based intervention displayed reduced activity in the brain regions associated with pain processing. This suggests that hope may actually alter the way the brain processes and interprets pain signals. It felt like the hope that epidural gave me drove my pain down from a 10 to a 6. And a 6, for me, was, well, manageable.

My friend Pastor Miles McPherson often preaches of hope, pointing to a famous 1950s study conducted by Dr. Curt Richter at Johns Hopkins University. Dr. Richter placed rats in a bucket of water to see how long they could swim before they began to drown. (You can think of it as like Navy Seal training, for rats.) Within minutes, the rats started sinking. Seconds before they drowned, Richter removed each rat from the water. He dried them off. He let them rest. Then, minutes later, he placed the rats back in the water. Round two: Let's see how long they last now. In the first go-round, no rat remained above water for more than 15 minutes. The second go-round? Remarkably, the rats swam for up to 60 *hours*.

Why? They had *hope*.

Richter concluded that the rats' ability to swim for so long on their second attempt in the water was due to the "hope" they had been given by being rescued on the first. That glimmer of hope gave the rats a renewed determination to survive, allowing them to push far beyond their previous physical limits.

I spoke with that second back deformity specialist armed with hope for the first time in a long time, too. And to my surprise, he, too, knew what I was about. "I know who you are," Dr. Greg Mundis said, politely, as he introduced himself.

You do?

He mentioned LaDainian. And Drew. He knew of Fitness Quest 10. And more so, of my keynotes, my speeches, and my podcast. Even my books: "You're the '*Get Your Mind Right*' guy... right?" I thought to myself, *I am. (Or, at least, I was.)* I remember thinking, *this doc did his research. I like that! I needed that.* Then we discussed my back. "You'll need surgery," he said.

Ugh.

"But Todd... you don't need surgery *yet*," he added. "You're not ready yet."

Say what?

In that moment, my pain nosedived from a 7 or 8 to a 4. I could deal with a 4. Heck, I could live with a 4. It was the exact opposite of when my pain shot up when I first laid eyes on that awful X-ray. "You're going to be fine," he stated matter-of-factly. Now that was the second—really, seventh—opinion I'd been searching for! He called a 14-hour surgery "ridiculous." And reassured me that when the time came for surgery, which it will come, he could fix me up in half the time. And in turn, cut my recovery time in half, too. Now *that* I could manage.

I'll always remember his name. Because he changed my life. Dr. Mundis minimized my pain, by *maximizing* my hope.

Body
Quarterback Your Healthset

My friend and fitness industry legend, Peter Twist, was diagnosed with stage IV head and neck cancer in 2011, when doctors pinpointed a tumor at the base of his brain stem. They found tumors in his mouth, too. And his throat. And his ears. The first oncologist "Twister" met with recommended palliative care, basically hospice, to ease him into the inevitable: Death. Twister said no. Then he met with a revolving door of oncologists, until he found one, *the only one*, that thought he had a chance.

That oncologist ordered a biopsy to determine a treatment plan. His team removed tissue from Twister's neck. Then the oncologist warned Twister, testing would take weeks. "Maybe a month." Time was of the essence, but they'd have to stand pat until then. It was out of the doc's hands. So Twister asked his oncologist a question: "Who owns the biopsy?" Sensing where the conversation was going, the oncologist smiled.

"You own it, Peter," he said. Twister stuck out his hand, then his oncologist handed him a small, sealed container containing said tissue. Twister immediately began contacting private labs until he found one that would investigate the biopsy that day and send the results to his oncologist that night. By quarterbacking his own health, Twister saved himself weeks. And maybe his life. It's an extreme yet effective way to illustrate my point: You must quarterback your own health. Doctors, oncologists, nutritionists, naturopaths, chiropractors, even personal trainers and coaches, all come from different backgrounds. And they all should have a spot on your roster. But it is critical that you determine who and what is right for you and that you lead the charge at each step. That's quarterbacking your health. And I know its power first-hand: That world-class radiologist. His praying nurse. Dr. Mundis. I may not have encountered any of them had I not quarterbacked my health.

Mind

Quarterback Your Mindset

Get your mind right. Just as you quarterback your physical health, quarterback your mental health, too. Here are just a few of my best practices to help you do so: Listen to positive podcasts (like my "IMPACT Show") as well as uplifting music or worship. Remember, what goes in your ears can boost what's between them. Avoid the news, negativity, and energy vampires to protect yourself. Go on gratitude walks, as I suggested earlier. And, of course, journal. I journal twice a day (sometimes more). If you want my personal prompts, get my "IMPACT Journal" to guide you. Read the good stuff, too. I personally aim to read two books per month. If you want more tips and tricks to quarterback your mindset, crack open my previous book, *Get Your Mind Right*, this month.

Soul

Quarterback Your Soulset

Get your soul right. Prayer, scripture, and service, are of course, options. But quarterbacking your soulset doesn't necessarily require religion. For example, I fuel my soul every morning by fueling someone else's through a little best practice I call the "Power of One." Every morning, I ask myself: *Who should I pour into today? Who needs me? Who needs my juice? My energia? My thoughts? My prayers?* I pinpoint that one person, then I pour into them.

Nowadays, it's often an encouraging text. "Hey, Joe. Thinking of you, brother. Make it a great day!" Or even a video or hand-written note. (Who doesn't love receiving a hand-written note? Heck, I collect them on my gratitude wall.) Are you game to try the "Power of One"? Who are you going to pour into today? Who needs you? Find that one person. Then type out a short, encouraging text, film a quick video, or whip up a letter and send it to them.

7

Presence – The Final Diagnosis

January 2022 – July 2023

Let's recap: 2018 was rough. 2019 was worse. 2020 was the worst year of my life. Then 2021 came along and said, "You ain't seen nothing yet." But by January 2022, my relentless pursuit of relief paid off: My back pain had mostly subsided—sans surgery. It'd been more than three full years since I felt that good, physically. The inevitable flare-ups felt almost like a tickle. After all, my back was still curved and my discs were still gone, but the flare-ups were comical compared to the pain that flooded my body throughout 2021.

Forget my back. *I'm back, baby!* Back in my zone, my element. My tail was wagging faster than Jersey's as we got back into walking. And for me, working out. But why? Better yet, how?

The hope Dr. Mundis (and others) gave me helped. It drove the pain down. Way down. I wondered what else helped: The hyperbaric chamber? The peptides? The cortisone shots? The meds? The massage? The stem cells? The countless clinics… and the countless treatments? The prayer? The stillness? The silence? Or simply time? Was it a coincidence? Was it divine healing? Was

True Strength

it a miracle? As others have said: "Don't question a miracle; just say thank you." So that's what I did.

But my guess is, it was probably the synergistic effect of all the things. The 1886 painting *A Sunday Afternoon on the Island of La Grande Jatte* by Georges Seurat illustrates this perfectly. Celebrated as a landmark masterpiece of the 19th century, today the painting is housed in the renowned Art Institute of Chicago, a testament to its enduring significance and acclaim.

What makes *A Sunday Afternoon* so special is its structure. The sprawling painting was created using the pointillist technique, where countless small dots of pure color blend in the viewer's eye to create images and shades. Said differently, the entire painting is composed only of dots. Millions of them. The dots on their own? Underwhelming. The dots together? Extraordinary. That's the synergistic effect in action.

Georges Seurat, *A Sunday Afternoon on the Island of La Grande Jatte*, The Art Institute of Chicago

Presence – The Final Diagnosis

We see it in chemistry and pharmacology. Business and economics. Sport and music. Even in supplementation. For example, curcumin, a compound found in turmeric, is known for its potential anti-cancer properties. The problem with curcumin is that it is not easily absorbed by the body, rendering it almost useless on its own. However, when you consume curcumin with black pepper, the black pepper increases the bioavailability of curcumin by up to 2,000%. Suddenly, unleashing its health benefits and unlocking its potential anti-cancer properties. Again, the synergistic effect; the whole is greater than the sum of its parts.

But now what? What's next?

2022 ended up being a blur. And I'm not saying that metaphorically. I barely remember the vast majority of the year. Here's the little I do remember: I was a mental mess. Like a punch-drunk boxer. Walking around as though concussed. Irritable. Forgetful. Foggy. Fatigued. Exhausted. So exhausted. I'd go to bed tired. And wake up every morning thinking, *I'm exhausted. I can't wait to go back to bed!*

What a conundrum. My back pain was virtually gone, but why didn't I feel right? Why didn't I feel like "me?" As my man Pastor Steven Furtick says, "You can be on your way up, and still have to deal with being down." That's how I felt. And I wanted to know why. I needed to know why.

Then, in early 2023, amid this secret, year-long battle stumbling through a mental maze of exhaustion, fatigue, brain fog (and perhaps a pinch of depression), the answer hit me like a ton of bricks: Chronic traumatic encephalopathy (i.e. CTE). *Oh, no.* The thought of CTE made my stomach drop. It built a lump in my throat. It made the hair on my neck rise. It made my spine tingle. Yet... it made perfect sense.

LaDainian's teammate, Pro Football Hall-of-Fame linebacker, Junior Seau, died by suicide in 2012. He shot himself in the chest at just 43 years old. It's been said he shot himself in the chest, and not the head, to protect his brain so that it could be studied. Perhaps he suspected he was battling CTE. Nine months later, after scientists studied his brain, Junior was diagnosed with, you guessed it, CTE. I remember grimacing at the headlines: "NFL's Junior Seau had brain disease CTE when he killed himself."

CTE is linked to repeated head traumas like concussions. Guess what? I had five *recorded* concussions in my playing career. And that's when documentation was up for debate. It wouldn't be all that surprising if I'd had several unrecorded concussions, too.

In a groundbreaking Boston University study from 2020, researchers found players with confirmed CTE were 10 times more likely to have played football for more than 14.5 years. And for every additional year played, the odds of having CTE increased by 30% per year. I played tackle football for exactly 20 years.

I thought of football legend and nine-time Pro Bowler "Iron" Mike Webster. After all, it was his brain that sparked the concussion crisis. Shortly after his playing career ended in 1990, Webster started exhibiting strange behavior that swelled into disturbing behavior over time. He was constantly lethargic. Irritable. Angry. Off. He peed in the oven once. He slept under city bridges. When his teeth fell out, he stuck them back in with super glue. Partially due to his lethargy, I'm sure, he'd zap himself with a taser to sleep. Mike died in 2002, at age 50.

In 2022, I was even training a client, a former All-Pro NFL athlete, who was demonstrating the startling signs of CTE before my eyes, in real-time. We trained three times a week for months

Presence – The Final Diagnosis

on end. And three times a week, a driver brought him to the gym, so he wouldn't get lost. I'd have to guide him to the water fountain in almost every session. And reintroduce him to people he'd met many times before. He could remember and recount specific details from decades ago, during his playing career, but he couldn't recall what he had for breakfast just hours earlier. It was hard to see. Hard to watch. Hard to fathom. I felt for him. This was a sharp man, suffering through advanced CTE right before my eyes. And as you can imagine, his struggle scared the heck out of me. We weren't far apart in age. And we'd both played the same game for a long time.

Every time I trained this client, uncomfortable thoughts filled my head: *Is this what's next for me? Am I a few years away from what he's going through? Weeks away from it? Days away from it? Is this God foreshadowing my future? Is this me... right now?*

Of course, I then began to recognize suspected symptoms of CTE in me: Lethargy, for sure. I had every excuse in the book to be tired, given the past few years. But this was excessive. It was uncomfortable. My memory was off, too. Like I said, 2022 was a blur. I wasn't angry, necessarily, but I was irritable. I remember journaling about it. It was affecting me as a parent. I suddenly had little patience with the kids. It was even affecting me as a husband—and that terrified me. Plus, I wasn't sleeping, at all. The bottom line is, I was off. I already had degenerative back disease... now did I have degenerative brain disease?

Wait, wait, wait, T. You're overanalyzing. You must be.

Flow... I let my emotions flow from my fingertips onto a questionnaire in 2023. A private SWOT (Strengths, Weaknesses, Opportunities & Threats) analysis of me and my current situation, as part of a lead-up to a private "Brand Mastery" event

I'd been invited to, hosted by *New York Times* bestselling author Rory Vaden. Here are just a few excerpts from that document, excerpts I categorized under T—Threats: First and foremost, "My health. My energy." I'm "frustrated. Stressed. Overwhelmed." I literally wrote, "I'm off." Followed by "I hate this feeling." I had so much to be grateful for, yet I felt like I couldn't catch a break.

And if anything, I held back a bit. I didn't go into detail about how down I was really feeling. I didn't, for example, mention that dash of depression I'm sure I was battling. Why? Because I was unsure if my SWOT analysis would be shared with others. And if so, with who? I had a reputation to maintain.

It felt like it'd been years since I attended an event *live*, particularly as a participant. Most were canceled in 2020. I couldn't move in 2021. And 2022 was a blur. But even after completing my homework, I wasn't totally sold on going to the event. After all, I was too tired, too lethargic, to fly across the country, from California to Nashville, Tennessee. I was so drained I was contemplating backing out. Even leaning toward it.

But if I didn't go, I'd be a hypocrite. Point blank. I couldn't forget something I'd been preaching from stages—physical and virtual—since the very beginning: "Show up and *be in the room*." No matter how tired I was, now that I was physically capable, I needed to "show up." I needed to be "in the room." So I forced myself on that flight to Nashville. And during our first break inside "The W" hotel, a(nother) doctor introduced herself: Renowned physician, Dr. Gabrielle Lyon. She had read every painstaking word of my SWOT analysis—and she wanted to help me.

"Stick out your tongue," she said as she inspected my mouth. "Turn your head." I did, as she looked at my ears. "How big is your neck?" she asked.

Doc, I thought to myself, *what's going on here?!* She seemed so determined, I felt obligated to reply. "17.5 inches," I said.

She asked a few more questions about my health history. And my family's history. Then she looked me in my eyes. "Todd...," she said. "I read everything you wrote in your SWOT analysis. I know that your ambition, motivation, and desire to inspire is still inside of you. I don't know if you have CTE... but what I do know is this: You have sleep apnea!"

Huh? I laughed. She didn't. I thought she was joking. *Isn't sleep apnea for the obese? Or the elderly? C'mon, Doc. I'm not that old!* Dr. Lyon went on to explain sleep apnea to me. Turns out that both conditions—CTE and sleep apnea—share strikingly similar symptoms: Excessive fatigue. Occasional memory lapses. Irritability. Mood swings. And so on. In both cases, your brain literally shrinks, too. Sleep apnea is no laughing matter. And per Dr. Lyon, I fit the profile. The shape of my tongue. The size of my neck.

I told her about my snoring—the snoring Melanie has complained about for years. Dr. Lyon told me that when I start snoring, I've probably stopped breathing. Sleep apnea is characterized by repetitive apneas during sleep. An apnea is the complete interruption of breath for at least 10 seconds. "If you don't breathe, you die," she said. That about took my breath away. Both are killers. CTE, the silent killer. Sleep apnea, the not-so-silent killer.

The National Sleep Foundation reports that untreated sleep apnea can increase the risk of high blood pressure by 140%, heart disease by 30%, and stroke by 60%. Per renowned psychiatrist Dr. Daniel Amen, sleep apnea triples the risk of Alzheimer's disease. Plus, it's linked to a litany of other serious health problems including irregular heartbeat, diabetes, and depression. In fact, patients with severe sleep apnea die on average 10 years sooner than those without. The kicker? Up to 90% of cases go undiagnosed.

As I learned about the severe consequences of untreated sleep apnea, I couldn't help but think of my father. I bet Dad had sleep apnea—and didn't know it. After all, he used to snore like a bear. And he struggled with his weight; he was 260 pounds. But sleep apnea wasn't widely recognized until 1993. Dad died in 1992. While I can't be certain, I strongly suspect that years of untreated sleep apnea may have contributed to his untimely heart attack and ultimately, his death.

Back in San Diego, the testing began. My local doctor confirmed Dr. Lyon's suspicions after analyzing a single night of sleep (or lack thereof). "Todd, you stopped breathing 120 times last night... for somewhere between 20-52 seconds each time!" On the night in question, I stopped breathing about 20 times an hour, or every three minutes. No wonder I felt so dull, tired, and lifeless. I was a walking zombie! "Your blood oxygen levels dropped to 75-79% with each apnea." Those kinds of dips in oxygen strain the heart and if left untreated, can open the door to other severe health complications that could ultimately lead to death. "That's why you're exhausted," the doctor said. "And it's been going on for years."

After my initial shock wore off, I was, in a weird way, relieved. Really relieved. Perhaps I *finally* knew what was wrong, why I was so "off," and most importantly, how to fix it.

Soon after, I was fitted for a CPAP mask—picture Maverick's mask from *Top Gun*. I strapped into my version the very first night I received it. The mask sealing my nose and mouth to deliver a steady stream of pressurized air through a tube that snaked to

Presence – The Final Diagnosis

the bedside machine. That pressurized air would keep my airway open and prevent pauses in breathing (apneas) during sleep.

And just like that, I felt *amazing*. Like a decade younger overnight. That mask, Dr. Lyon's diagnosis, flipped the switch. It turned me back on. In what felt like a single night, that year-long fog clouding my every waking moment and thought in 2022 finally dissipated in July 2023. I sprang out of bed, alive again, and lit up like a Christmas tree. *Let's go, baby!*

Later that morning, my right-hand man Larry Indiviglia scooped me up. Though I wasn't scheduled to take the stage, I was feeling too good to miss out on the Super Bowl of fitness conventions—IDEA World in nearby Los Angeles. I knew my peers would be shocked to see me there as a participant (and not a speaker). But the truth is, I had not even considered requesting to speak back when applications were due months prior. Remember, I was in far too much pain then, and buried in far too much brain fog, to seriously consider an event, or speech, of any kind. And even if I had managed to sneak onto the schedule, how would I traverse the crowds? Get up on stage? And deliver the kind of high-energy, heart-thumping keynote I'd become known for?

Now, as I slid into Larry's car, I could barely contain myself. "Larry, I'm back!" I hollered. The words tumbled out, my voice brimming with a childlike excitement I hadn't felt in ages. For too long, I'd been hiding the pain, masking the truth that drained my energy and passion. Only I knew how much those two words—"I'm back"—truly meant.

As of that moment, in July 2023, armed with my brand new CPAP machine, I was officially back in the game. I was living again. The burn-out. The closures. The death threat. The leap. The surgery. The back pain. The soul-searching. The sleep apnea.

Suddenly, it was all in the past. Finally, I could see the sun through the clouds and the forest for the trees. Finally, I had the juice, the energia, to find what was next.

But why?

Because I showed up in Nashville, Tennessee. Because I showed up, period. It all goes back to showing up. It all goes back to being "in the room."

Days after IDEA World in July 2023, my friend Travis Barnes and I started talking about my next "wave"—my next soaring crest, which I'll share with you shortly. But here's the thing: If I hadn't showed up in Nashville, if I hadn't been in the room with Dr. Lyon, I'd still be in a daze. I'd still be stuck in a valley. Or even worse, the not-so-silent killer could have left me dead.

Body

Get Off Your "But"

I met Sean Stephenson in 2017, and we hit it off right away. Sean was born with osteogenesis imperfecta—otherwise known as "brittle bones" disease. The doctors who delivered him warned his parents that their baby boy would be dead within his first 24 hours of life. He lived until he was 40 years old. However, his bones were so brittle he suffered an incomprehensible 208 fractures by just 18 years old. Sneezing would break ribs. Putting on pants too quickly could snap a femur. On top of that, his rare condition left him just three feet tall, 45 total pounds, and confined to a wheelchair.

Yet, Dr. Sean Stephenson, also known as "the Three-Foot Giant," became a therapist, a self-help author of multiple bestselling books, and a world-renowned motivational speaker who traveled the world speaking on stages. But how? If he could barely put on pants without the risk of injury, how could he safely board a plane? Traverse a venue packed with tens of thousands of people? How could he get there, let alone present? The answer: He showed up.

Sometimes it took up to five different strangers to pick Stephenson up and transport him to his next stage. But he'd be there. He always showed up. To quote Stephenson and his book title, *Get Off Your 'But.'* Your "but" being your excuse to *not* show up. The "buts" that weigh you down. The "buts" that weigh us down. Sean Stephenson had at least 208 excuses to not be in the room... but he always showed up. What about me? What about you? When you get off your "but" and show up... good things happen.

Mind

Be Where Your Feet Are

The Dalai Lama said, "Man sacrifices his health in order to make money. Then he sacrifices money to recuperate his health. And then he is so anxious about the future that he does not enjoy the present, the result being that he does not live in the present or the future; he lives as if he is never going to die and then dies having never really lived." In other words, be where your feet are, my friend. Be in the present. Because your presence matters. Showing up, physically, is step one. Showing up, mentally, is step two. Don't just be there. Be present.

Soul

Stay in the Game

Dr. David Jeremiah always shows up for our training sessions. The one time he didn't, he called me from the hospital: "The devil is trying to take me out of the game," he said. "But I won't let him." My friend, the devil wants to take us all out of the game—including you and me. Don't let him.

I believe the devil does his best work at three critical moments in time: 1) Right before something big, a big project, game, event, you name it. In Dr. J's case, the devil pounced right before the highly anticipated release of his 2023 book, *The Great Disappearance*. And like he told me over the phone, "The great disappearance won't be me." 2) When you're at your weakest. Physically. Mentally. Spiritually. Or all three. I know that from experience. 3) Following a big win. Remember, the crest of the wave determines the depth of the valley. But no matter what, show up and stay in the game.

That's the only way to win.

8

Essence – What's Next?
2024

"He or she who has their health has one thousand dreams. He or she who does not... has one." Ain't that the truth. I think I said that quote a thousand times *prior* to 2020. During that string of deflating years from 2020-2023, I had just one dream: Get my health back. Win it back. Even if it took a miracle.

The historic Commonwealth Games of 1954 featured two of the most celebrated middle-distance runners of the time, Roger Bannister of Great Britain, and John Landy of Australia, facing off in what would become a legendary race later dubbed "The Miracle Mile."

A few months prior to "The Miracle Mile," both athletes had accomplished a feat that was once thought impossible—breaking the four-minute barrier for the one-mile run. Bannister was the first to do so on May 6, 1954, running a mile in 3 minutes 59.4 seconds. Landy broke Bannister's record less than six weeks later, on June 21, 1954, with a time of 3 minutes 57.9 seconds. Their record-breaking feats set the stage for the epic showdown between the two at the Commonwealth Games that August.

Landy led "The Miracle Mile" for most of the way, setting a blistering fast pace. However, as the runners approached the final lap, Bannister began to close the gap. With just 90 yards or so to go, Landy glanced over his left shoulder to gauge Bannister's position. And at that exact moment, Bannister overtook him on the right and went on to win the race. This split-second glance, known as "Landy's Look," became a pivotal moment in sports history and is immortalized in a bronze statue of Landy looking over his shoulder at Bannister.

After looking back for so long, having won my health back by 2024, I was finally able to look forward again, to turn my head and focus on what was in front of me. Although I do believe in the power of reflecting, as "Landy's Look" and subsequent loss proved, you will get passed up if you stay stuck in the past—or stuck in reverse. Said differently, your dreams must be bigger than your memories.

Ever since that back injury shattered my dream of being an NFL quarterback in 1996, my dream, my goal, my mission has been to IMPACT 10 million lives. Between leading hundreds of fitness professionals, delivering countless keynotes, creating a library of products including multiple books, and of course training clients at the mothership, Fitness Quest 10, I believe I've done that. My right-hand man, Larry Indiviglia, is sure of it. He's done the math to prove it.

"How Todd has already impacted 10 million people in 15 Years"
by Larry Indiviglia

TODD DURKIN MASTERMIND

TD MASTERMIND INSTITUTE LEVEL –

Todd coaches an average of 60 people every year and each of these people impact 15 people in their daily walk and life:
> 900 people x 15 people = **13,500** people

Each of these 13,500 people impact 15 people:
> 13,500 people x 15 people = **202,500** people

Each of the 202,500 impact 15 people:
> 202,500 people x 15 people = **3,037,500** million

TD MASTERMIND PLATINUM LEVEL –

On average, there have been 4 teams of 15 people, each coached by a Platinum Coach. Each coach impacts 15 people:
> 4 coaches x 15 people = **60 people**

Each of these 60 people impact 15 people:
> 60 people x 15 people = 900 people x 15 years = **13,500 people**

Each of these impact 15 people:
> 13,500 people x 15 people = **202,500 people**

Then each of the 202,500 impact 15 people:
> 202,500 people x 15 = **3,037,500 million people**

> **TODD KEYNOTES**
>
> Workshops and Presentations: 40 per year with an average of 300 people per event:
> 40 keynotes x 300 people = 12000 people x 15 years = **180,000 people**
> They, in turn, each impact 15 people:
> > 180,000 people x 15 people = **2,700,000 million people**
>
> **BOOKS**
>
> 4 books written = 60,000 books sold and each book impacts at least 15 people per book:
> > 60,000 books x 15 people = **900,000 people**
>
> **TRAINING**
>
> 15 years x 100 (training sessions) per month:
> > 18,000 sessions x 20 per session = **360,000 people**
>
> **TOTAL = 10,647,060 people impacted by Todd Durkin!**

So what's next?

In my darkest moment, Melanie challenged me to dream bigger. Her wise words are forever ringing in my ears, like a song I can't get out of my head: "What if 10 million is just the beginning?"

Those words challenged me to find new purpose in my pain. To turn my burden into my blessing. To use my back as a vehicle to multiply my dream. To impact *100 million* lives, as she suggested. This new dream, as you can see, is far bigger than my old dream, just as the windshield is far bigger than the rearview mirror. Therein lies the problem: How could I impact 100 million

ESSENCE – WHAT'S NEXT?

lives with just one facility? With just one Fitness Quest 10? I couldn't. I can't.

In 2024, on the other side of all those valleys, I wrote in my journal, "Happiness is the journey to the next thing." And guess what? I (finally) found "it." I committed to "it." The next thing. The something more. The something different. The something even greater. The something I'd been searching for. The something the whispers spoke of. Yes! I found the way, or wave, to accomplish my new dream of impacting 100 million lives: "IMPACT-X Performance."

On March 17, 2024, exactly four years after I was forced to temporarily close Fitness Quest 10 due to the pandemic, I signed an agreement naming me the CEO of my new fitness franchise: IMPACT-X Performance. A brick-and-mortar franchise that specializes in delivering fitness, recovery, life-coaching, and faith—all under one roof! YEP!

These nationwide human performance facilities go beyond the scope of traditional fitness to nurture strong bodies, minds, and souls. Each facility is lit up with positive energy, incredible community, and like-minded people from all walks of life—each is a place, *the* place, where you can find, forge, and foster *your TRUE STRENGTH*. And boy, oh boy, I couldn't be more excited to see you there!

With the sweep of my wrist on that agreement, I suddenly felt that same boyhood excitement that I hadn't felt since 1999, when I signed the lease for Fitness Quest 10. Ironically, I never wanted multiple facilities. I never wanted more than just one Fitness Quest 10. In fact, I turned down the opportunity to *franchise* more than once. Just as I said no to *TRUE STRENGTH* once before, I said no to franchising as well. Then, in 2024, I said yes to both.

I believe, just as my near half-decade journey healing my first back injury equipped me to lead Fitness Quest 10 (and impact 10 million lives), I believe my near half-decade journey through the valleys revealed in this book—my journey finding, forging, and fostering *my TRUE STRENGTH*—has equipped me to lead IMPACT-X Performance (and impact 100 million lives).

I can't tell you how good it feels to know I am where I'm supposed to be. Doing what I'm supposed to be doing. I've never been more excited about the future. Today, I'm more inspired by where I'm going than where I've been. Not only am I "back" in the game of fitness, I'm on a crusade to change more lives than ever. When I say the best is yet to come, I mean it. I believe it. I don't know what the future holds. For me or for you. Here's what I do know: Without the valleys, nothing changes. With them, you become stronger. You dream bigger. They equip you to experience something more. Do something different. Accomplish something even greater.

Arthur C. Brooks, Harvard's "Happiness" Professor and the author of the *New York Times* bestselling book *From Strength to Strength*, calls it the "second curve." The second curve refers to the idea that after reaching the peak of one's professional or personal achievements—often accompanied by traditional markers of success like prestige, income, and influence—individuals can experience a decline in happiness or satisfaction if they continue on the same path without change. Brooks argues that to sustain happiness and a sense of purpose beyond this peak, individuals need to embark on a second curve. That's me, baby. That's IMPACT-X!

IMPACT-X PERFORMANCE

The late, great John Wooden, the "Wizard of Westwood," led the UCLA men's basketball team to all 10 of his NCAA championships after age 53. Guess how old I am as of writing this (and signing on as CEO of IMPACT-X Performance)? Yep. For me, I believe this second curve is, in fact, my next crest. I believe the next 25 years will be my best 25 years. And I believe my next crest will be my best crest. After all, the depth of the valley determines the crest of the wave. Therefore, the best is yet to come—for you and for me.

Body

Swim

From atop a stage, Sean Stephenson asked the crowd, "Do you know how rescue teams choose who they are going to save when a helicopter approaches an ocean of drowning people?" Do you? Picture this: A helicopter hovers above a wreck in the middle of the untamed ocean. The pilot has a bird's-eye view of survivors literally fighting for their lives. But as the helicopter inches closer and closer, he looks down and realizes there are more people in the water than space in the helicopter. Who do they save? Who would you save? Their motto is "We can only save the people who swim toward us."

In some ways, this is represented in the logo for IMPACT-X Performance. It's the lighthouse, guiding the way. Lighting the path. A place to swim to whether you're at the top of the crest—or floundering beneath a breaking wave. But remember, you are the X-factor. You must swim. You must swim to it. Your next wave, the next crest, life's best crest, won't scoop you up if you are sitting on your hands.

Mind

"Iron" Michael Chandler's Affirmation and My Favorite Quote

Many times over the past several years, when it felt like life kept punching me in the face, and knocking me to my feet, I thought of fighters, warriors, others who had been glued to the mat, and rose back to their feet. I'd picture Rocky Balboa, then hear Sylvester Stallone's deep, gravelly voice speak my favorite quote that hangs inside of my home-gym:

"The world ain't all sunshine and rainbows. It's a mean and nasty place and I don't care how tough you are, it will beat you to your knees and permanently keep you there if you let it. You, me, or nobody is gonna hit as hard as life! But it ain't how hard ya hit. It's about how hard you can get hit and keep moving forward. How much you can take and keep moving forward. That's how winning is done!"

I thought of a mantra, or affirmation, as well, that my friend and client, three-time Bellator MMA champion and top UFC fighter Michael Chandler speaks of. Win or lose, "Iron" Mike repeats the following three things to himself post-fight: 1) My family still loves me. 2) My God still loves me. 3) I still love me.

Ain't that the truth! No matter who you are, or what you believe, the hardest part is often the third one: Loving yourself isn't always easy. But you, my friend, are the X-factor. The X in IMPACT-X symbolizes the number "10," because at IMPACT-X, we analyze 10 aspects, or markers, of your health, to deliver tailored training. But the X also represents *you*. Because when it comes to *TRUE STRENGTH*, you are the X-factor. Keep swimming. Keep fighting. The world needs you at your best. You need YOU at your best.

Soul

The Candlelight Taoist Parable

An old Taoist master was asked by a student how to find enlightenment. The master lit a candle and handed it to the student, saying, "This candle represents your inner light. To find enlightenment, you must keep this flame burning brightly, even in the darkest of times. Share your light with others, and never let it be extinguished."

Since I was young, I've always been enamored with lighthouses. Enamored with the light. That's why I'm so excited to have lighthouses—i.e. IMPACT-X Performance facilities—across the nation. Our light will be burning brightly. Inviting you to shine yours. And I hope you'll do just that. When things are dark, go to the light. And always shine yours.

9

Faith – Connecting the "Coincidences"

2024

I remember regularly scribbling scripture until my wrist went limp, searching for meaning in the suffering. Albeit extreme at times, I now know how effective it was. But I couldn't always see it then. It was like trying to diagnose a storm in the middle of a tsunami or reading a book while riding a rollercoaster. Impossible. But boy, hindsight is 2020. Only when you've reached the end can you look back and see that the winding path you took was, well, that perfect. No different from a river carving canyons through solid rock, it's only after the canyon has been formed that we can step back and marvel at the landscape.

Now out of the valleys, above the canyons, I often imagine myself up in the clouds. Looking down on my life. A fittingly God-sized view of His God-sized plan. And that's when I see it. That's when I think to myself: *Danged, God. Was this all part of Your plan?*

"Our calling is revealed in God's timing, not ours."

Faith is believing when you cannot see. I see that so clearly now. I've had that realization or revelation. That otherworldly "aha" moment. I see the connectedness of the coincidences. The "God winks" as I call them. You know, those little gestures, those tips of the cap from the man upstairs, those anonymous coincidences that surely must be more than just coincidence. (As others have said, "Coincidence is God's way of remaining anonymous.") Just as when you listen, you can hear the whispers. When you look, you can see the signs.

For example, Kim Parker came in for Pilates at Fitness Quest 10 in 2003. Then she dragged her husband in. Towering Mr. Parker was *the* Vaughn Parker, the 6' 6" 320-pound starting left tackle for the San Diego Chargers. Vaughn led me to LaDainian, who led me to Drew, and so on. I only ended up in San Diego because it was as far as my run-down car could take me after Michael King of King World Productions (the production and syndication company behind Oprah, Jeopardy, and Wheel of Fortune) brought me to L.A. Then on my very first day in grad school at San Diego State University, guess who I met? Melanie Hardiman... my future wife. Three days before I was scheduled to spend 72 hours with Dr. Daniel Amen to face the music and be evaluated for CTE, I met Dr. Gabrielle Lyon in Nashville, Tennessee—who diagnosed me with sleep apnea. Mere days after my friend Travis Barnes, who I had been coaching through my Mastermind group for more than a decade, first approached me with the idea of franchising, Jeff Fenster—the founder of one of the nation's fastest-growing franchises, Everbowl, as well as WeBuild, a company that serves as the single source of procurement, manufacturing, fabrication, installation, and construction for other franchises

Faith – Connecting the "Coincidences"

and concepts—walked into my life and offered to advise me on franchising. *Are you kidding me?*

Of course, the biggest coincidence of them all starts and now continues with my back. "It looked like life as I knew it was over," I told the newspapers, reminiscing on my journey to Fitness Quest 10 after my back injury in the 90s. "But, in hindsight, (my broken back) was the pivotal point in my life, almost a crossroads." My broken back, as I mused to the media in the early 2000s, was the catalyst of Fitness Quest 10, my vehicle to impact the lives of 10 million people. And now today, my back issues are once again serving as the catalyst for IMPACT-X Performance, my vehicle to impact the lives of 100 million people. Another God wink. Another "coincidence." Here's one more: The title I turned down, *TRUE STRENGTH*, is now the one that I believe will have the most impact.

My blessings are countless. And in my heart of hearts, I know there are more to come. The best is yet to come. I know this to be true from the cathartic connection of these coincidences that can only be seen from the clouds—that 35,000-foot view. There, with that God-sized view of my 53-year journey, I see a masterpiece. I see how each piece of the puzzle fits so perfectly together. Forget my plan—I see His plan is bigger. Way bigger. And way better. Even when it knocks me off my feet. And I see something else, too: The valleys and the crests. They're all connected. No different from a mountain range. It is in the connecting of the coincidences that I see the connectedness.

Pastor T.D. Jakes says, "The blessing is often in the broken. For every time you were broken, you multiplied." (Or as Dr. J says, "It's good to be broken every now and then... because that's how the light gets in.")

On the other side of this journey, of the valleys we just traversed together, the light was let in and my dreams multiplied. I multiplied. But so did something else: My faith. Already a man of faith, I probably have prayed more in the past four years than I did in the previous 40. In the car next to Melanie, my co-pilot. In Tijuana, tucked inside that hyperbaric chamber. In Cabo, from that cold, hard floor. In North Carolina, immobilized in a bed.

My prayers were rarely answered at the moment. I didn't always hear that whisper, that "yoo-hoo." But looking back now I see it, I feel it; my faith continued to grow. To multiply. So often we turn to prayer, or faith, in times of darkness, in times of despair. And now, today, with two surgically-repaired knees and a spine that looks like a question mark, I feel stronger than ever—because my faith is stronger than ever. It carried me through the tough times. The further I went down, the more I connected with what's up, what's above.

"You don't have to just pray when things are bad; pray when they are good as well."

When your body or mind are wrong, the lynchpin, the secret ingredient, the black pepper to the curcumin, is faith. Faith is the most important "protective factor" of *TRUE STRENGTH*. It's faith in God's plan. (Heck, that's why IMPACT-X Performance is the first health and fitness franchise to specialize in delivering fitness, recovery, life-coaching, and faith under each roof.) If you ask me, He sits atop the depth chart in the game of life. We can see to the corner. God sees around it. The religions may be different. And that's OK. But each of us needs faith. After all, being is believing.

> *"Your biggest weaknesses may make the biggest impact in the world."*
> Psalm 139

At least once a week, someone asks me: "When are you going to open up a church?" Well, as Pastor Jeremiah would say, "Everything you do is a ministry." Here's the point of this sermon, to you, the reader: Have faith because you're going to need it. When you're blinded by pain, walk by faith, not by sight. Remember, it's all part of a bigger, better plan.

Body
Don't Wait to Listen

Atop Mount Horeb, also known as Mount Sinai, a place of great significance as it is where Moses received the Ten Commandments, Elijah seeks God's guidance. God tells Elijah to stand on the mountain, and then, per the Bible (1 Kings 19:11-12 (NIV)) a series of dramatic events unfold: "Then a great and powerful wind tore the mountains apart and shattered the rocks before the Lord, but the Lord was not in the wind. After the wind there was an earthquake, but the Lord was not in the earthquake. After the earthquake came a fire, but the Lord was not in the fire. And after the fire came a gentle whisper."

Think about that. Despite these impressive displays of power, God's presence is not found in the wind, earthquake, or fire. Instead, Elijah encounters God in a "gentle whisper," also translated as a "still small voice" or "soft whisper." This passage suggests that He guides, He communicates, in quiet, subtle ways rather than always through dramatic, overpowering means. Elijah, seeking God on Mount Horeb, finds Him not in grandiose displays but a gentle whisper, illustrating that divine presence and guidance often come in quiet, subtle forms, not just dramatic revelations.

To me, that's faith. It's not a religion, it's a relationship. Like fitness, like exercising, the magic doesn't always happen in the moment. The growth, the strength, develops over time. My faith used to be so much of talking to God. Now it's far more about listening to Him. Why not start listening now? Why not start building, or strengthening, your belief, your faith muscle, now? Don't wait. Don't wait for a prognosis, a diagnosis, an accident, an injury, a divorce, a split, a crisis, a burden, burn-out, or a new, deeper valley, to start listening. Listen to the whispers today. Listen for that "yoo-hoo." And if you're already listening, listen more intently. Listen closer. Keep diving deep and tapping into the whispers. Ego shouts, God whispers.

Mind

Put on Your "Armor"

In the midst of this challenging journey, my inner circle tightened. One of the small groups I grew closer with were the guys and gals in my weekly Bible study group led by Miles McPherson and his wife, Debbie. The group included Pro Football Hall of Fame wide receiver Andre Reed and his wife, Theresa. NFL wide receiver Tyrell Williams and his wife, Searra. Plus, award-winning actor Chad Michael Murray and his wife, Sarah.

Chad equates his faith to armor. Spiritual armor. Check this out: "I feel stronger and safer walking onto my sets every day knowing that I have God with me," Chad says. "When you have that comfort that you just feel safe, you feel different, you feel the opportunity to handle more, your shoulders are bigger, you can carry more weight. (That's why) I get up every day and I put that spiritual armor on... then get ready to go to work."

Like Chad, faith gives me strength—even at my weakest. As the Bible states, "When I am weak, then I am strong" (2 Corinthians 12:10). The bigger the battle, the bigger the eventual blessing. If you saw its size, you'd understand the magnitude of the battle you're fighting. You're gonna need your "armor." So put it on. And get to work.

Soul

Footprints in the Sand

A famous Christian allegorical poem goes as follows: "One night I dreamed a dream. As I was walking along the beach with my Lord, across the dark sky flashed scenes from my life. For each scene, I noticed two sets of footprints in the sand, one belonging to me and one to my Lord. After the last scene of my life flashed before me, I looked back at the footprints in the sand. I noticed that at many times along the path of my life, especially at the very lowest and saddest times, there was only one set of footprints. This really troubled me, so I asked the Lord about it. 'Lord, you said once I decided to follow you, You'd walk with me all the way. But I noticed that during the saddest and most troublesome times of my life, there was only one set of footprints. I don't understand why, when I needed You the most, You would leave me.' He whispered, 'My precious child, I love you and will never leave you. Never, ever, during your trials and testings. When you saw only one set of footprints, it was then that I carried you.'"

As lonely as I felt at times from 2020-2023, I was never alone. He's always with us. He's always with you, even when you feel alone. Your faith, your belief, He, can carry you to success—even when you fail. Because He will not leave you or forsake you. When flesh and blood fails, God will not.

I know this to be true.

And Then Some

And then some. Those three words, that mantra—one of many I live by—is indicative of conquering the extra mile. Going above and beyond. The final 1%. That additional degree that transforms standing water into a boil. The cherry that tops off the sundae. That's what this chapter is dedicated to: And then some. The people, places, and things that gave me that extra nudge, that final push, the "and then some" to find, forge, and foster my *TRUE STRENGTH*. The people, places, and things that will help you do the same.

Body

You Are Who You Surround Yourself With

Your quality of life is directly related to the quality of people you surround yourself with. They rub off on you. On how you act. On how you think. On what you believe. And what you do. Or as Proverbs 27:17 states, "As iron sharpens iron, so one person sharpens another." Who's sharpening you? Who are you sharpening? And who *should* you be sharpening?"

During this journey, there were several people who shined their light on me. Who gave me light. Who served as lighthouses, helping to guide me out of the darkness, out of the valleys. Like me, you have these people too. Lighthouses. Godsends. Angels. Whatever you want to call them. I'd like to take a moment to acknowledge several of mine.

1. **Julie Wilcox:** The one and only "Mama Jules!" "Juju." You've been by my side for 19 years, both at Fitness Quest 10 and Todd Durkin Enterprises, touching tens of millions of lives—including mine. Thank you for being a lighthouse to me and everyone that, together, we impact.

2. **Larry Indiviglia:** Larry, I'm not letting you go anywhere. Your thumbprints are all over this book—and my life. Just as they should be. I love you, brother. Thank you for being the man you are and for being by my side. Everybody needs "a guy." You're him.

3. **Pastor David Jeremiah:** It's not lost on me how lucky I am to have you in my life. I don't take a single session for granted. Dare I say there's been no man who has impacted me more in the past decade. You're a true icon of our generation—and I'm proud to call you a friend and mentor.

4. **Drew Brees:** From talking ball to talking life, thanks for being part of my inner circle and introducing me to yours. There's nobody else I'd rather be on this "second curve" with. Not only am I pumped to see you enshrined in the NFL Hall-of-Fame in the near future, I'm excited to see your impact on humanity in this next phase of life. If I'm Mickey, you're my Rocky, brother. We keep each other "sharp."

5. **Kelli Watson:** You're one of the best coaches and people I know... period. An absolute Godsend, and I recognize how blessed I am to have you in my life. Together, we'll keep creating impact—through Scriptor Publishing, our coaching programs, and what's next. Thank you for being YOU.

6. **Jeff Bristol:** My partner in Fitness Quest 10. You were the right guy, at the right time. Thanks for being by my side, in the "fox hole" with me, through the thick and thin. And thank you for keeping the Fitness Quest 10 legacy alive (we're not done yet!).

7. **Travis Barnes:** My partner in IMPACT-X Performance. After a decade-plus of coaching and mentoring you, I am so fired-up for what's about to come next and the IMPACT we are about to create for millions of people.

8. **Pastor Miles McPherson:** Our weekly Bible studies were my escape. My reprieve. My sanctuary. Thank you for strengthening my faith when I needed it most. For over 25 years, you have had massive impact on my faith. But none have been more important than the last few. Thank you, my friend!

9. **Tom "Dex" Dexter:** My William & Mary teammate, friend, financial advisor, and strategic advisor. It's been an honor to be on the same "team" as you for more than 35 years. I'll never forget you attending my dad's funeral in '92. And I never will. You're family, brother. We are about to create some serious impact together. Love ya.

10. **Chase Daniel:** Thank you for helping to keep Fitness Quest 10 financially afloat during the darkest days of the pandemic. I was blown away by your unprompted generosity. I still am. I'm also honored to call you a client and a friend for over 15-years. Thank you for being YOU. Love ya, brother.

11. **Joe Pangelinan:** I see your *TRUE STRENGTH*. I feel it. I benefit from it. Thank you for living with incredible IMPACT and inspiration while fighting for your life. You inspire me, brother.

12. **Warren Roark:** I bared my soul to you during all this. You're really the only one who knew *everything* going on besides Melanie. Heck, you may have known even more than her. Haha. Thank you for being a best friend now for 30+ years. I believe that without our near daily talks and accountability to each other... well, I hate to think of the alternative. Thanks my man. Love ya, WAR!

13. **Melanie:** You're the bookends of this book for a reason: You hold *everything* together... and have done so for our 23 years of marriage. Through every peak and every valley, you've remained an incredible wife and life-partner, the best mother to our kids, a world-class leader to your students, and a faith-filled servant. You hold us together. You hold me together. I'm excited to see what God has next for us. Thanks for being you. I love you, Melanie.

Mind

Find Your Sanctuary

We all need a sanctuary. The Homestead in Whitefish, Montana, has become that special sanctuary for me. What's your sanctuary? Where's your sanctuary? Maybe it's the beach. Or the lake. Research has shown that spending time near bodies of water, like the ocean, can have positive psychological effects. Scientists call this the "blue space effect." Maybe it's a cabin in the woods. A study by Ulrich et. al. (1991) found that patients recovering from surgery in rooms with a view of nature had shorter hospital stays, required less pain medication, and reported fewer complications compared to those with a view of a brick wall. Imagine that.

Maybe, like me, your sanctuary is in the mountains. Or climbing them. A study by Atchley, Strayer, and Atchley (2012) found that individuals who spent four days hiking in nature, disconnected from technology, showed a 50% increase in creative problem-solving abilities compared to a control group. The bottom line is, you need to find that place where you can unplug. Step away. Where your soul can sing. And who knows what might walk into your life?

Soul

Serve Your Scars

The more you serve, the more your soul sings. The more your soul sings, the more you want to serve. I create to serve. I never created more new things—products, programs, content, etc.—than I did during the tough times revealed inside this book. The truth is, I feel like I do my best work under pressure. Or, in pain. I believe coming from a place of pain empowers you to do your most purposeful work.

My friend, your suffering, whatever that may be, is of service. Your scars are signs of strength. Survive your scars now so you can serve through them later. Because as my friend Rory Vaden says: "You are most powerfully positioned to serve the person you once were." Or like my friend and fitness colleague Denise Druce said on my podcast, "Serving your scars allows you to be a better person and ultimately create more impact." Amen.

Though difficult, I needed to share this story, my *TRUE STRENGTH*, for me. For my healing. But its purpose is to serve you. Like its predecessor, *The IMPACT Body Plan*, *TRUE STRENGTH* is a product of pain. I hope it helps heal yours. As Muhammad Ali said: "Service to others is the rent you pay for your room here on earth." Please pay it forward. Share this book, share your *TRUE STRENGTH*, with someone in need. And when you need a hand, you know where to find me—either at my beloved mothership, Fitness Quest 10, or popping into one of my many nationwide "lighthouses," IMPACT-X Performance. I encourage you to do the same. Come to your local lighthouse. Because together, we can reach 100 million.

The 31st Lesson

Let's face it: My back is still "broken." My spine is still warped. My discs, gone. While I'm out of pain now, I recognize that punishing back pain could return at any moment. I recognize I will, at some point, likely need major back surgery. I also recognize I, like you, will face more valleys. Different valleys. Greater valleys. Perhaps my pain pales in comparison to the pain you're going through. Or the pain you've been through. Your valleys may be physical. They may be mental. Emotional. Financial. Relational. Even spiritual. Yet at the same time, I believe the best is yet to come for you and for me.

In each of the nine chapters leading up to this moment, I revealed a "protective factor" of *TRUE STRENGTH*: Rest, Gratitude, Growth, Perspective, Stillness, Hope, Presence, Essence, and Faith. I also shared three hard-earned lessons with you to help you find, forge, and foster each factor: One for the body, one for the mind, and one for the soul. The final lesson, the 31st lesson, is this: *The best is yet to come.*

Remember that. As I've told my children since the day they were born, and as I reinforced to myself at my lowest moments detailed in this book, "Always do your best... and never give up." Always keep going. Because on the other side of every valley is a crest. And I now know this to be true.

My friend, I hope you'll use this book, and the 31 hard-earned lessons I've shared, to find, forge, and foster your *TRUE STRENGTH*, so that you, too, can climb up and out of any valley you face—and reach that next crest. I hope you'll begin to forge and foster your protective factors starting today, starting now. So that they are always with you, ready to be leveraged when you need them most, and arming you with the healthset, mindset, and soulset, the eccentric strength, your *TRUE STRENGTH*, to rise from the valleys, so you can enjoy bigger and better crests. From the bottom of my heart, thank you. And Amen.

Much love... and much IMPACT.

The best is truly yet to come!

A Note from the Co-Author

Clay Manley

Beaming, Todd greeted me with an ear-to-ear smile and a bone-crunching bear hug. It'd been several years. He looked older, wiser, and... shorter? He sounded different, too. Though positive, less Pollyanna. Upon reading the first draft of this book, my wife, Kelli, pinpointed it: It's not age. It's edge. (Our agreement to co-author this book had a death clause. How's that for edgy?) I continued writing and revising... embracing that edge. But something else struck me as I analyzed piles of personal journals he kept during the times detailed in this book: Todd's faith. It was everywhere. More abundant than ever before. We began every meeting, and there were many, with prayer.

You see, I accepted this project on the heels of a massive life change, a cross-country move from California to South Carolina (it was like moving from one planet to another, entirely different, planet). That move was followed by a series of painful events that thrust me into an emotional state. An emotional state that served me well while writing. On December 12, 2023, the afternoon before the bear hug that kicked off this project, my phone buzzed: A fellow father and a close friend of 20+ years, Dave Benalcazar, was calling... with tragic news. Dave had been diagnosed with eye cancer out of the blue. A few short weeks later, my phone buzzed again. Dave wanted to Facetime. *This has gotta be good news*, I thought. *Yes! No.*

Dave was cloaked in a hospital gown. Resting on a gurney. His eye wasn't the root issue, just a symptom of a much larger and much scarier issue. Dave had just been diagnosed with stage IV lung cancer. He hadn't smoked a day in his life. Worse, the aggressive cancer had already spread from his lungs to his brain, bones, and liver. He and his fiancée, Alyssa, were forced to schedule a shotgun wedding, just in case, you know… something happened. Chemo, radiation, the works, it all began less than 48 hours after they wed.

Soon after Dave's tragic diagnosis, my friends Hank and Pam Ebeling lost their 15-month-old son, Henry. The frantic text message Hank sent sharing the news still haunts me. I can only imagine the pain they were forced to endure (and continue to endure). In our new neighborhood in South Carolina, 4-year-old Adam longed to play with his "fwends" again after six months of crippling cancer treatments confined him to the house. Dave began cancer treatment the day after his 36th birthday. Camila, another local child, was forced to begin chemotherapy the day after her third birthday party. Everyone has something. And those are just a few of the harrowing valleys I witnessed and people I prayed for, with Todd, while writing this book.

But then a crest: "Can you whistle?" Dave's oncologist asked out of nowhere. Dave pursed his lips; a squeak filled the air. "That's your lungs," the oncologist whispered to Dave with a smile. "Clean as a whistle!"

A Note from the Co-Author

Writing this book was a crest for me. And I wish for more crests. For Dave. For Alyssa. For their son, Ezra. For Hank and Pam. For Adam. For Camila. For me. And for you.

To your next crest,

Clay Manley

P.S. I'd like to thank several folks who made this book better by bringing out the best in me: Thank you to my wife, Kelli, for your honesty, your love, and your perspective. Thank you for being the glue that keeps me together. And thank you for catching me in the valleys and leading me to countless crests.

Thank you, Mom, for being my best editor and the most patient and understanding human I know. Thank you, Dad, for my discipline, my work ethic, and the chip on my shoulder. Thank you, both, for 36 years of crests. Thank you to my brother, Chris, for being a sounding board for me as an author and an inspiration for me as a father. Thank you, and R.I.P., to my twin brother, Michael; you are a constant source of motivation.

I hope my words make each of you proud.

Thank you, Dave, for your *TRUE STRENGTH*. I saw it in your eyes the day after you were diagnosed. Thank you for our Facetimes, our "daily doses." And for 20+ years of friendship. Thank you, Kevin, for the cart rides. For listening. And for setting the temperature. Thank you, J.R. Moehringer, for your indirect inspiration. Thank you, Justin Prince, for transforming me into an author. Thank you, Todd, for trusting me to help translate your message for the masses.

And thank you to my son, Weston: You light up my life, bud. Nothing beats coming home to a warm hug and your beaming smile after a grueling day of writing (or a frustrating day struggling to write). You give me *TRUE STRENGTH*. I love you so much, son.

About Clay Manley

Clay Manley is a proud father, Simon & Schuster-published author, and prize-winning copywriter and marketing consultant on a bold mission to co-author 10 *New York Times* best-selling books alongside his next 10 clients. His work has earned accolades from the American Writers & Artists Institute (AWAI), Forbes, and Inc. 5000. And his words have been endorsed by world-renowned leaders, entrepreneurs, and athletes including *New York Times* bestselling author John C. Maxwell, international keynote speaker and entrepreneur Justin Prince, and ultra-endurance athlete and Ironman world record-holder James "The

Iron Cowboy" Lawrence. A native of Wheaton, Illinois, and a graduate of Indiana University, Clay now lives in Summerville, South Carolina with his wife, Kelli, their son, Weston, and their cat, Frankie. For inquiries, contact Clay@ClayManley.com. For insight and inspiration, follow Clay on Instagram at @Clay.Manley.

About Todd Durkin

Todd Durkin is an award-winning strength, conditioning, and mindset coach, internationally recognized motivational speaker, bestselling author, and entrepreneur. He's known for his body, mind, and life-transforming work as a coach and confidant to top business and religious leaders, renowned entrepreneurs, and elite athletes including Super Bowl champions, World Series champions, X-Game gold medalists, and Olympic gold medalists. Durkin is the founder of Fitness Quest 10, a human performance facility regularly named one of America's Top 10 Gyms, as well as the Founder and CEO of IMPACT-X Performance, a cutting-edge brick-and-mortar fitness & coaching franchise that specializes in fitness, recovery, life-coaching, and faith—under each roof. A sought-after speaker, Durkin has delivered more than 300 keynotes across five continents, hosts an award-winning podcast, and has authored four bestselling books. He is a dedicated family man, married to his wife, Melanie, for 23 years, and a proud father to their three children: Luke, Brady, and McKenna. The Durkin family is completed by their beloved golden retriever, Jersey.

CONNECT WITH TODD

Website:
www.ToddDurkin.com

Social Media:
IG: @ToddDurkin
FB: www.Facebook.com/ToddDurkinFQ10
Linked-In: @ToddDurkinFQ10
YT: ToddDurkin
X (formerly known as Twitter): @ToddDurkin

FREE Weekly Motivational Messages:
Additionally, please sign-up for Todd's FREE motivational & inspirational weekly messages and videos that he will send to your phone and email.

By signing up today, you will receive exclusive content and messages, be able to ask questions directly to Todd, and you will be in his "inner circle" of communication & motivation.

You can SIGN-UP for FREE by doing the following:
1. Simply text "True Strength" to (619) 304.2216
2. OPT-IN at www.ToddDurkin.com

INVITE TODD DURKIN TO SPEAK TODAY

Todd Durkin is a dynamic keynote speaker who loves inspiring those seeking high performance and maximum success in their life. He has spoken all over the world to a wide array of audiences in a multitude of industries.

As one committed to creating a massive impact, Todd has a passion to instill a championship mindset in people of all ages, levels, and sectors. He has a knack for tapping into people's mindsets and heart-sets to help them reach their full potential personally and professionally. His passion, contagious positive energy, and ability to connect with all audiences allow him to routinely receive standing ovations and rave reviews.

If you, your business, your conference, your college or university, or your organization would be interested in having Todd speak (Live or Virtually) on TRUE STRENGTH, GET YOUR MIND RIGHT, IMPACT, or to customize his message for your audience,

please contact him through his website:
www.todddurkin.com/Speaking

TUNE INTO TODD'S WEEKLY PODCAST

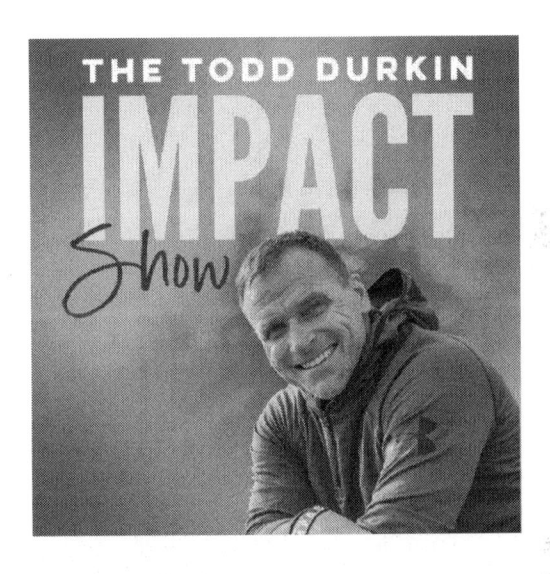

The Todd Durkin IMPACT SHOW is designed to motivate and inspire you to live a life full of passion, purpose, and IMPACT. It's guaranteed to **Get Your Mind Right**!

The IMPACT Show is for anyone who seeks high performance in business, health, fitness, sport, leadership, or life.

Available Wherever You Get Your Podcasts

IMPACT-X PERFORMANCE

Founded in 2024, IMPACT-X Performance is an innovative & holistic fitness business looking to shine light around the country. Led by fitness legend, Todd Durkin, we are bringing the methodologies and strategies that have sculpted the bodies, minds, and souls of some of the greatest pro athletes in the world, to YOU.

This gym franchise incorporates 4 pillars: Fitness, Recovery, Life-Coaching, & Faith.

We currently have 6 locations in operation around the United States (NY, PA, NH, IN and soon to be Huntington Beach, CA).

Will you be the next?

For even more information on how to be a part of our "IMPACT-X Performance" community, check out www.impactxperformance.com.

Made in the USA
Middletown, DE
02 February 2025